Tiffany Norris

is a no-nonsense mummy concierge, journalist and pregnancy guru who has worked with hundreds of pregnant mothers, and supports every woman who needs her help with tips and guidance – and sometimes just a listening ear.

She was a journalist and presenter for Mumsnet, has written for *Cosmo* and *Grazia* and is an expert for The Baby Show. Tiffany runs 'Mummy Masterclasses', parenting workshops for soon-to-be and new parents. She was the winner of the prestigious Jacqueline Gold Women in Business award and has won the Theo Paphitis Small Business award.

You can find her @mummyconciergehq on Instagram where she would love to hear from you.

Secrets of the Mummy Concierge

Parenthood just got a whole lot easier . . .

Tiffany Norris

BLINK
bringing you closer

First published in the UK by Blink Publishing
An imprint of Bonnier Books UK
The Plaza, 535 King's Road, London SW10 0SZ
Owned by Bonnier Books
Sveavägen 56, Stockholm, Sweden

www.blinkpublishing.co.uk

facebook.com/blinkpublishing
twitter.com/blinkpublishing

Paperback – 978-1-788-703-95-6
eBook – 978-1-788-703-96-3
Audiobook – 978-1-788-703-97-0

A CIP catalogue of this book is available from the British Library.

Typeset by IDSUK (Data Connection) Ltd
Printed and bound in Great Britain by Clays Ltd, Elcograf S.p.A.

1 3 5 7 9 10 8 6 4 2

Blink Publishing is an imprint of Bonnier Books UK
www.bonnierbooks.co.uk

This book is dedicated to my world: Rupert,
Ophelia and Baby Number 3 (due July 2021!).
'Whole wide world, little ones.'

Contents

Introduction:
Vagina Casts and Photo Shoots

It's 9am on a Monday and I'm chatting to a client about vaginas. Or, to be more specific, *her* vagina. And if it will ever be the same again . . . Before you start guessing, no, I'm not a doctor, midwife or sex therapist. I'm something completely unique: A Mummy Concierge.

It's not unusual for me to start my day dealing with someone's nether regions. Sometimes it's explaining exactly how it might feel to push a baby out through it (you've heard the watermelon and nostril analogy, right?). Other days, it's lamenting the fact that our vaginas will never be the same again, post tiny human popping out through them.

But today is something completely new. Even for me.

'Do you think the make-up artist needs to sort things out . . . down there?'

Marcia is a client who I have been working with for a total of nine months now. She is currently sitting awkwardly on her hospital bed with what I suspect is a large sanitary towel between her legs and a couple of stitches. We are in the exclusive private maternity unit of one of London's most prestigious women's hospitals and there is a two-hour-old baby lying contently on her chest.

1

Two make-up artists plump, contour and highlight every centimetre of her face whilst a hairstylist spritzes and puffs every one of the auburn hairs on her head. Fake eyelashes are applied, bronzer is 'whooshed' across temples and Crème de la Mer is slathered onto arms and legs.

Behind me, a clatter of photographic props are being assembled – a collapsible light reflector is balanced (much to a midwife's horror) on the side of the baby's bedside cot, a tripod with a second camera is being nervously manned by the photographer's assistant and an intern is brandishing the latest iPhone and snapping a 'behind-the-scenes' video, which I have no doubt will shortly appear on Marcia's Instagram page.

On the surface everything looks like a magical magazine shoot. A mother and her baby, contentedly drinking in the new world around them and staring at each other with amazed wonder at their new life together. The hospital room is filled with Jo Malone reed diffusers (which I placed there two hours previously) and every tabletop and windowsill is adorned with fresh flowers and family photos of holidays to the Alps.

But Marcia is not a celebrity, nor is she a social media influencer. In fact, she is just a new mummy and one of my first client. But hey, what mother wouldn't hire a team of stylists and photographers to document their first baby? Oh, right . . . just Marcia then?

'STOP RIGHT THERE. DO NOT MOVE. THIS IS THE SHOT! THIS IS THE ONE!'

I am shoved to one side and narrowly miss landing in a pile of blood-soaked sheets (the midwife hasn't removed them yet) as Martin, the photographer, bounds past me and pushes his camera in Marcia's face: 'COME ON, BABY! JUST ONE LITTLE SMILE FOR UNCLE MARTIN. YOU CAN DO IT!' Martin speaks in capitals. Every word, I have come to realise, is shouted at the top of his voice regardless of the delicate situation he might be in (*has he noticed the sleeping baby?*).

I see the frustration form on his face as the baby, as yet unused to glamorous photo shoots – probably due to the fact that she is less than 24 hours old – dribbles slightly, then squeezes her eyes even more tightly shut. Marcia looks down at her little bundle and sighs. I can't work out if this is in shared frustration with Martin or if it's a sigh of contentment and happiness at being a new mother – let's go with the latter.

'Tiffany, you didn't answer my question.' Marcia is looking up at me expectantly. 'The make-up artist . . . Does she need to make up my vagina?'

It's at this precise moment that my world turns from slightly surreal to, *OMFG, is this my actual job?* Marcia lifts up the sheets and reveals (to everyone in the room, no less) the damage that has been done down below. Above the hospital bed sheets, we have a scene punctuated with designer nightdresses, scented reed diffusers and Ibiza chill-out music pumping lazily from the radio. Below, there is blood, amniotic fluid and a swollen, purple vagina ravaged beyond recognition to something resembling a hamburger.

If ever there was an Instagram vs reality photo, this would be it.

Let's backtrack to four days ago. Marcia, who I have been working for since the day she found out she was pregnant, sent me a slightly cryptic text, which simply said, 'Vagina cast, pre-baby. Thoughts?'

I typed back cautiously: 'Great idea! What are you thinking?'

Her reply came back instantly. 'It's Nigel's 50th just after the baby's due date, so I thought a great gift could be a cast of my vagina . . . *pre*-baby. That way, he can remember what it looked like before it's ruined forever and replicates the aftermath of World War I. Thoughts?'

Marcia always ends text messages with the single word, 'Thoughts?' We both know she doesn't actually mean it. My thoughts are irrelevant, especially when it comes to her intimate regions, but I humour her nonetheless.

'Great idea! I'm sure he will love it. I'll start looking into it for you now.'

A text bounds back before I have even finished writing:

'And a photo shoot. Literally AS SOON AS THE BABY IS OUT! I want make-up artists, hair stylists, the whole shebang. Can't have my Insta announcement tarred with photos of a tired mummy and ugly baby.'

My pen swirls over my notebook: task number two – photo shoot immediately after birth.

'And whilst we're on that,' her text continues, 'I need a hashtag for when I eventually give birth. Something that

4

might start trending. #NewBaby is just so passé. Get on it for me, will you?'

Number three on the to-do list: birth hashtag. Can't be passé.

You might think Marcia is just a one-off example of the type of client I deal with on a daily basis as a Mummy Concierge.

You'd be wrong.

* * *

My name is Tiffany Norris and I am The Mummy Concierge. I run a 24/7 full-service Mummy Concierge business in London for what I like to call 'The Million-Pound Mamas'. I work with mums who are going to spend thousands upon thousands of pounds on nursery for their kids (even though all they are going to do is finger paint) and max out their platinum cards on maternity wear (that they will throw away after nine months). I'm a concierge catering for my clients' every need, no matter how quirky or impossible.

By the way, the vagina cast isn't even the most extreme thing I have done for my clients. I've tracked down a breast pump in North America at 4am, found a £1,000-a-day Lego therapist for a two-year-old, flown halfway across the world to 'babyproof' a holiday villa and even named a child. As in, created a baby name that has never been used before (or likely ever again).

The parents called her 'Moxy' for those of you who are wondering.

Becoming a mother can completely catapult your life into something new and unnerving, so I was determined to make my role as a Mummy Concierge a 'lifeline' for any other mummies out there. I wanted to be the person they could turn to when things got tough, the fount of knowledge on everything there is to know about baby buggies and zip-up baby grows. Acting as a baby's personal assistant, on-call therapist and social director, I set out to be the ultimate peacekeeper and negotiator when it comes to bringing a new tiny human into the world. I can tackle anything, from decorating a nursery with vegan paint to hiring a stylist for an unborn child. Believe me, there's nothing I can't (or haven't been asked to) do.

But it's not all glamour and baby grows. As with any life-changing event, being pregnant and having a baby brings with it roller coasters of emotion, moments of complete desperation and an innate need to make everything, in the words of Mary Poppins, 'practically perfect in every way' from the word go. So, welcome to the world of The Mummy Concierge. Now, take a deep breath – because you're about to see a completely new side to motherhood.

Love,
Tiffany

PART ONE

PREGNANCY

Chapter 1

Patrick and I had been married for less than two months in 2012 when I was given the opportunity to have a free 'Fertility MOT Test'. At the time I was working as a freelance journalist for *Cosmopolitan* magazine when an email from a publicist jumped into my inbox with the subject line, 'Can you actually have a baby?'.

To say the subject line intrigued me was an understatement. I was used to receiving emails from PRs offering me glamorous (and sometimes not-so-glamorous) freebies in return for coverage in a national magazine. However, this email was different: it was as though the PR had seen inside my psyche. The night before, I had been out at a work event and a conversation came up about marriage and babies.

'Why do people, the second you get married, start asking when you're having a baby?' Julia, a fellow journalist, shouted to me as she swiftly downed a tequila shot. 'It's like saying, "tick tock . . . you need to have animalistic sex tonight and create a mini human being and then tell us all about it".'

I laughed and the conversation moved on. It had been short and sharp, but it had a lasting effect. That night, I went home and hesitantly asked the question I had been too nervous to ask my husband before.

'Patrick?' I reached over and nudged his heavy, sleeping body.

'Tiff, it's 2am! What do you want?'

'Do you think now we're married, we should have a baby?'

I think that got his attention. He sat up swiftly in bed and turned on the bedside light.

'We got married a week ago, Tiff. What's the sudden urgency?'

He was right, of course. Even my father had told me on our wedding day to 'enjoy time, just the two of you' before we had children. So, with that, and a tummy filled with tequila, I too rolled over and forgot about it. Married life had only just started, we were going to enjoy it for a bit.

The following day, the email arrived. My curiosity piqued, I responded swiftly, saying I'd be happy to do a Fertility MOT for *Cosmo* and write about the experience. I justified it to Patrick as a way of encouraging women to look after themselves and get a health check. A week later, we were standing on Harley Street in central London, full of trepidation and excitement.

I never thought for one minute the results would come out as they did.

'Your fertility is pretty low.' The doctor didn't lean towards me or offer a reassuring shoulder rub as he said this. Instead, he closed his file, beckoned for his assistant and told her to get the details for IVF treatment. Patrick and I sat next to each other, a dull silence vibrating off the walls as we digested what had just been said. The tears slipped silently down my nose as the doctor's assistant handed me a leaflet detailing IVF treatment. Patrick glanced at it briefly, but I saw his shoulder stiffen. The man I married was never going to give in without a fight so, as the assistant tried to push an IVF leaflet his way, Patrick took my hand and 'demanded' another option.

'Well, we can do some more tests. Some invasive, some not.' The doctor shrugged his shoulders, as if communicating nonverbally that he thought this would all be a waste of time regardless. I, on the other hand, saw his statement as a sign of hope. The adrenaline surged through my body. I had to do something – *anything*. Suddenly, becoming a mother was the most important thing to me.

I often think back to those days at school in the biology lab, dressed in squeaky new uniforms and clutching new pencil cases that were our pride and joy, giggly and embarrassed as we started our first sex education class. Drilled into our malleable little brains with absolute certainty was the fact that if you had sex, you would have a baby. But how wrong could that be? As I moved swiftly into adulthood, I had never considered that becoming a mother could potentially be something that was so hard to achieve. I had the formula right in my head – find a man, fall in love, get married and have children. That's what happens in all the great love stories, right? But sitting there, in that doctor's room, being told that my dream of motherhood might not be achievable after all, shattered everything I had ever seen my future as being. We all know sex can, of course, lead to babies, but in my case, it was looking more likely that in order to get pregnant, the 'conceiving' bit would take place via multiple tablets, injections, surgeries and the use of sterile equipment.

For all of my life, I had been focused on becoming a mother – I felt it was something that ran through my veins – but suddenly my focus had to shift. I had to actually be able to get pregnant for this dream to be realised. In my way now was a huge stumbling block: I was being told that it might never happen. However, I also came to a decision that day, as I stared back into the unsympathetic eyes of the doctor in front of me, as he handed me a price list of all the possible 'tests' we could do: if we were to go through something as stressful as fertility testing, I would not be doing it at this clinic. I needed to find someone else, someone who I could trust completely.

Being told you might struggle to get pregnant can really propel couples forward, and in our case it certainly did. Patrick and I made fertility treatment our main priority – for over two years we met with different fertility experts, I took various vitamins, had multiple tests and cried . . . a lot. My desire to have a baby now at the forefront of my mind, I began to open up to friends, slowly and hesitantly at first, to let them know what Patrick and I had been going through over the past couple of years. An old school friend,

Tara, was the one who, rather than wince at me and tell me 'to relax and it will happen', actually offered some advice that started to steer us in the right direction.

'I'm in the same situation,' she confessed, clasping my hand as she did so. 'Ted and I have been trying for a baby for years and it's not happening.' She then rummaged in her handbag and tore off a strip of paper from her diary, scribbling a name and number on it. 'Contact this lady. She's a fertility expert. If anyone can help, she can.'

I remember feeling like Charlie Bucket when he was handed the golden ticket to Willy Wonka's Chocolate Factory. For some reason – be it the urgent look Tara gave me as she handed me the contact details, or the fact that it was another 'golden thread' I could grasp at – I walked home to our flat feeling a sense of elation. THIS was going to be it! This woman would be the one to give Patrick and I exactly what we wanted.

A few days later, we arrived on the steps of the hospital. I had heard about it before – its name whispered amongst my wealthier friends as though it was a top-notch elite members' club – but I had never actually been there myself. At first glance, it was just like any other private hospital. Women clutching Burberry handbags and talking loudly into their mobile phones waited in the reception area. The air smelled of expensive perfume mixed with money. Patrick had already balked at the fees to see Sara, the expert, but we agreed that we would at least meet with her, talk about our situation and then go from there. We weren't going to commit to anything until we were 100 per cent sure she could help us.

As we waited to be called into Sara's office, I idly picked up one of the hospital brochures and started flicking through. My nerves were up in the air and I'd already scratched off half of my nail varnish, so I needed something – *anything* – to distract myself.

What I saw when I opened that brochure will never leave me. The hospital I was sitting in is well known for catering for wealthier patients. It is where everyone from Victoria Beckham to the Duchess of York has paid a premium for the ultimate 'luxury' birth. Having read the leaflet from front to back, I turned on my phone and began searching to find out as much as I could about the place where I was currently sitting. It is one of the top private maternity hospitals in Europe and, as a result, most parents-to-be end up spending around £30,000 to have their babies there. According to various news reports, over 16,000 women a year pay for the luxury hospital experience.

The more I read, the more frantic the butterflies in my stomach became. Here I was, in one of the best hospitals in Europe, about to see one of their top fertility experts. To me, my chances of having a baby suddenly seemed more viable.

And it was at this exact moment an idea popped into my head, too. Something to do with the idea of making parenthood as easy as it can possibly be . . .

Chapter 2

I've always been described as someone who regularly comes up with wacky business ideas. Five years previously, I had set up the UK's first Proposal Planning company, helping people propose to their loved ones in unique and creative ways. Everyone thought I was mad when I set it up, but it ended up taking the world by storm and I even had my own TV reality show, with a camera crew following me around as I planned out-of-this-world proposals!

And here it was, happening again. A business idea that I knew people would laugh about and raise their eyebrows in a *'Here we go, another one of Tiffany's mad business ideas'* way. But sitting in the reception area of the hospital, I was seeing a world unveil itself to me that I hadn't seen before. Here were people who were used to having the best and paying for it too. They were going to this hospital because it promised them a high-end, luxury experience when it came to having their babies. Where the hospital could offer incredible medical expertise, gourmet meals and luxury hospital suites for mothers in labour, I could suddenly see something that it didn't have – and that there was a need for. The woman sitting in the corner, idly flicking through photos of her latest holiday to the Maldives on her iPad. The woman who had just walked through the revolving doors, a neat little pregnancy bump encased in a Gucci minidress. A couple, both glancing anxiously at their Rolexes and scribbling down notes in their leather-embossed Smythson notebooks . . . They all needed something *more*.

These were people who were used to having everything they ever wanted at the click of their fingers. But where was the person who could help them when it came to preparing for their baby? Where was their own personal baby expert, who could advise on everything to do with becoming parents – from what baby equipment to buy and where to luxuriate on their babymoon to which obstetrician would hold their diamond-encrusted hands and make them feel safe?

These people needed a Mummy Concierge. They needed someone who was, essentially, their PA for parenthood. And as far as I could tell, there was no one in the world doing it right now. But there was one person, sitting not far away from them, determined to make it happen . . .

* * *

My first appointment with Sara, the fertility expert recommended by my friend Tara, came and went in a whirl. We were ushered into her office and the first thing that hit me was how 'unmedical' it all felt. Sara's office was more akin to what you might imagine the office of a fashion editor of a top women's magazine to be like. Huge vases full of pregnant-looking peonies were dotted around the room, their delicious scent filling the air. Immaculate watercolours hung on the wall – splashes of muted pinks, blues and greens displaying pregnant stomachs and elegant smiles. An enormous glass desk dominated the room, with a vibrant pink lever-arch file the only thing cluttering it.

Rather than the haggard-looking, tired physician I had expected, Sara looked as though she had just stepped out of Charles Worthington. Her red hair bounced around her shoulders and her silk blouse looked as though it had been plucked from a recent issue of *Vogue* – I'm pretty certain I caught Patrick drooling. But there was a professionalism about her that I immediately respected. She welcomed us, offered us a cup of coffee and then spent the next 70 minutes just talking. She asked us everything – what we had tried so far, what tests we had done, why other doctors had said we had a problem. Then she read through our notes and then re-read them. She called in her secretary and arranged blood tests and scans, all with the efficiency of someone who really understood and knew what she was doing. She was a woman in control and this was exactly what we needed. Not at any point during our first meeting, or in the countless others that followed, did she ever let us believe that we couldn't have a baby.

What followed were months and months of every test you could imagine. I had a HyCoSy (where you sit spread-legged in a doctor's chair whilst they push water up through your fallopian tubes in the hope of clearing them). The pain was so unbearable that the nurse whose hand I was holding actually yelped as I squeezed it to counteract the burning agony I was experiencing in my stomach.

Next came the Clomid tablets. These tiny little tablets are taken every day and 'trick' your body into increasing a certain hormone that makes your body release more eggs. The surge of hormones was so strong, one minute I was laughing uncontrollably at *X Factor* and the next, I was a crumpled heap of tears on the floor because we had run out of cat food. I had numerous transvaginal ultrasounds where a probe is inserted via your vagina, and underwent more than four attempts at intrauterine insemination (IUI) – where your partner's sperm is placed inside your uterus by a doctor in the hope it increases the number of sperm to reach the fallopian tubes and subsequently increases the chance of fertilisation. Nothing worked. And I got very good at crying.

It all took its toll on our relationship. No meal could be had without discussing fertility treatments. We no longer laughed at toddlers causing trouble when visiting friends, instead sighed inwardly and gave each other a look that became our constant: this wasn't going to happen for us, we just had to accept it.

Patrick wasn't immune to the testing either. He regularly had to go to the fertility specialist and was directed to a small room where he looked at dog-eared porn magazines and tried to 'produce' some samples that could later be tested. The humiliation of having to do this – as has since been confirmed to us by numerous friends who had fertility treatment too – is beyond explanation. Walking out of a room and handing a nurse what is essentially a test tube of sperm, whilst a man in the next-door cubicle does the same, is a dent to any male ego.

The arguments between us became more frequent and more brutal. I was convinced Patrick was looking at me in a new, dull light. I was no longer his wife and potential mother of his babies. I was a failure. Unable to produce an heir. I was tainted. It's worth noting here that Patrick NEVER felt any of these things. In the moments when I cried myself to sleep and confessed my fears to him, he would hold me tight and reassure me strongly that he never felt this way about me. In his mind, I was going to be the most incredible mother some day – it was just going to take us a while to get there.

As is the case when something happens that I can't cope with, I turned on my 'journalist' mode. Nights on end, I sat up googling and researching everything there was to know about fertility treatment. I read sob-inducing stories of women who were never able to become mothers and of mothers who lost their babies. Everywhere I looked, I saw women desperate to become mothers who were struggling like me.

Looking back, I know that this is the moment motherhood became all too real to me – because it was the first time I was actually faced with the prospect that I might never experience it. One night, whilst Patrick slept feverishly next to me, I pressed 'play' on my fertility hypnotherapy podcast (research had led me to believe that it might help) and heard the therapist say the words, 'help you to become a mother'.

It wasn't an impressive or distinct statement, but as I heard it, something clicked inside of me. I reached for the biro I always kept on my bedside table and scribbled down the words 'mummy help' on the back of an ASOS receipt. Then, as swiftly as that thought occurred, I forgot about it and downed another Clomid tablet.

Looking back, I suppose in that moment my brain had clicked again onto something wonderful, but my heart wasn't ready to digest it yet. I had realised that mothers out there needed help. I wasn't a doctor so couldn't help people get pregnant, but maybe I had something else I could offer.

Unbeknown to me, the idea of The Mummy Concierge had just been born.

Chapter 3

At this point in my journey to motherhood, it was over a year since we had met Sara. During that time, I had been through various rounds of IUI, taken more than 48 pregnancy tests, spoken with numerous fertility doctors and broken down in tears whenever I saw any pregnant or new mummy in the street. I wrote list after list about how life could still be good without being a mother.

Having had a horrific couple of months doing back-to-back fertility treatment, I was physically exhausted and Patrick and I both knew we needed a holiday to get away from it all and relax. A close friend of ours – knowing what we had been going through – offered us their farmhouse in Tuscany. When they sent us the photos, Patrick and I spent hours just gawping at them – the infinity pool that looked over the green and yellow Tuscan hills, the beamed kitchen with dried hydrangeas hanging from the ceiling, the covered terrace with vines heaving under the weight of the purple grapes . . . It looked perfect.

But the booking of our holiday also had a bittersweet twist to it. On the day we booked our flights, we also decided to put a halt to fertility treatments. My body (and my mind) had been put through too much and we were both exhausted from the emotional tiredness and unhappy expectations that met us every month when my period made an appearance. The cost of the fertility treatment was also adding up – so much so that I could see the pressure and stress on Patrick's face whenever we received a letter with the hospital address emblazoned on the top. All in all, we felt as if we had been sucked dry, financially and emotionally. And it was time for it to stop.

I constantly worried that the stress of trying to have a baby would pull apart mine and Patrick's relationship. Thankfully, it held strong, despite the fact that I had become obsessed with getting pregnant. Bit by bit, I was unravelling and losing myself. So, in February 2016, we stopped. Clutching another negative pregnancy test in my shaking, pale hand, I gulped away tears as I told him I couldn't do it anymore.

'Maybe we're not meant to be parents? Maybe it's just not supposed to happen to us?' Patrick stroked my hair to calm me down.

The conversation about ending fertility treatment was probably one of the most emotional we had ever had. Despite knowing, internally, that it was the right decision, I battled, sobbed and cried as Patrick listed all the reasons we needed to stop.

'Just look at your stomach, Tiff,' he said carefully, pulling up my T-shirt to reveal a tummy that was the colour of a bruised plum due to all the hormone injections. 'And then there's us . . .' He left the sentence hanging, knowing that I would understand what he was talking about without having to say any more.

We had definitely changed throughout the fertility process. Gone were the days when we would belly laugh at each other's attempts at doing foreign accents or jump at any opportunity to do something spontaneous. Instead, we had been replaced by a couple who did everything by the diary – every appointment, every day of the month, was mapped out on our phones and in our diaries so that we knew when/if/how I was ovulating. Sex was no longer something we did for fun, it was now a pre-arranged, static event that happened for the pure purpose of trying to get pregnant. The arguments came thick and fast – I was obsessed with everything to do with babies and found myself unable to talk about anything else. Even on days when we went for a walk through Hyde Park to clear our heads, I would spot happy families or newborn babies being pushed around in prams, and end up in a fit of tears.

The blame also made an appearance at my more vicious moments, where I bandied words around, such as, 'Go and find someone who CAN give you a baby' or 'Maybe it's you', followed by a challenging stare meant to make Patrick feel inferior and the reason for our troubles. The sad fact is, looking back now, it was neither of our 'fault'. It's something I remain very passionate about, that infertility should never have a finger pointed at one person in a couple. Blame and resentment is the one thing that can kill a relationship – but especially a relationship where getting pregnant is at the forefront of the couple's minds. The only way Patrick eventually managed to convince me to stop with the fertility treatments was to promise me we could register under the NHS for IVF. We knew that having IVF on the NHS was likely to take a lot longer (due to the huge waiting lists) so we decided to take a break for six months and hopefully by the end of those months, we would get a call from the NHS, telling us we could start.

The day we booked the holiday, Patrick headed off to his office and after answering a few work emails, I decided to start sorting through my 'holiday wardrobe' in the hope of mustering up some enthusiasm about our Italian getaway in a few weeks' time. Goodness, that sounds so spoilt, but I have to acknowledge that there was a sadness there too. We had stopped all treatments and my dreams of becoming a mother seemed to have had a full stop put next to them. As I picked up a little summery dress to throw into my suitcase, I pulled it across my stomach and breathed in deeply, making my tummy protrude and look as if I was pregnant. It was as though I was punishing myself, saying, 'You could have been pregnant on this holiday and looked like this . . . but you're not.'

I knew my period was due to arrive whilst in Italy, so rather than delay the inevitable, I decided to quickly do a pregnancy test to be sure. There was not one single iota of my being that thought I was pregnant. The sole purpose of me doing that test was so that I wouldn't spend the first couple of days in Tuscany having the occasional 'hope' that my period might not arrive. I wanted to be organised and devoid of disappointment, so I quickly peed on the stick and then went back to my packing. Two hours later, and my suitcase was full. I'd also managed to spill the entire contents of a red nail varnish on the white carpet (Patrick was going to go mad!) so I quickly rushed into the bathroom to grab some tissue in the hope of mopping it up. Seeing the pregnancy test on top of the loo cistern, I grabbed it idly, glancing at it quickly whilst simultaneously unravelling loo roll from the holder for the nail varnish.

I then collapsed on the bathroom floor.

The test was one of those slightly newer brands that tells you a) if you ARE pregnant (with a very obviously, digitally typed-out 'pregnant/not pregnant' announcement) and b) works out how pregnant you are in weeks. Mine read as follows:

Pregnant. 4–6 weeks.

My first thought was *How?* As far as I could remember, our sex life had gone down the drain having decided to stop fertility treatment. We had been so used to scheduling sex by the clock that we had actually been enjoying just getting into bed and going to sleep, rather than checking our diaries or having me emerge from the bathroom waving an ovulation stick. Yup, sex had become a process rather than something we lost ourselves in and, as such, we had forgotten the positives of it and actually enjoyed, er, not having to do it!

However, miracles do happen. And in our case, they obviously had.

My next thought was: *Do I really want this?* I know that sounds strange coming from someone who had been trying for a baby for so long, but when it actually happens, your mind does strange things. Suddenly I was pining for the life I had left behind – the boozy Saturday nights sitting in a friend's garden in the summer, the tight-fitting jeans that showed off my stomach, the ability to just jump on a plane or visit friends abroad without having to plan. Your brain really does do strange things when you find out you are pregnant and I'm not afraid to admit it. But it's only now, on reflection, I can see why I was thinking things like this: I was scared. Petrified, even. Here was something I had been longing for, for so long, and it had actually happened. I was scared of how life was going to change. Scared in case something went wrong with the pregnancy. Scared how Patrick would react. Scared I might not be a good mother. Scared in case the baby wasn't healthy . . . It was at this precise moment I now realise I 'became a mother'. Why? Because when you become a mother, fear engulfs you. You are suddenly in charge of a brand-new, innocent and fragile life and keeping that little one alive and healthy and happy is your responsibility.

An hour later and I had managed to compose myself a little. I still had mascara stains under my eyes and I had peed on four more pregnancy tests. I sat in our tiny little spare bedroom (God knows why I chose this room for our announcement, but it seemed the most comforting in its tininess), waiting impatiently for Patrick to arrive home. All five pregnancy tests were now positioned under a pillow on the bed and I'd been googling 'How to tell your husband you're pregnant' for the last 40 minutes. In the end, I downloaded a pregnancy app and calculated my due date (7 May 2017) before taking a screenshot on my phone.

Patrick ambled through the door at 5.20pm, chatting away on his mobile on a work call. I watched him walk past the spare room (unaware that I was huddled on the floor) and into the kitchen. I heard the fridge door open and close, and him ending the call. He then called my name:

'Tiff? Where are you?'

'In here . . .' I uttered meekly.

He walked in through the door looking confused, a bottle of sparkling water in his right hand.

'What are you doing in here?' He gave me a quizzical look and came and sat next to me. 'All OK?'

This was the moment. I handed him my mobile phone and told him to look at the screen.

'Cool,' he said, registering the photo. 'Who's pregnant?'

He didn't think for one minute it could be me. Instead, he stood up as though to walk away, sighing heavily. I forgot sometimes that the lack of children was hard on him too, that he felt utter deflation on finding out another of our friends was pregnant whilst we were still barren.

'It's not a friend,' I whispered to his back, the air getting caught in my throat as I did. He turned around in slow motion and saw me remove the pillow from the bed, revealing the five positive pregnancy tests. 'It's me.' The words tumbled from my mouth and the tears followed. 'We are having a baby. I'm six weeks pregnant.'

Believe it or not, I had been due to start IVF the following week, when we returned from our holiday.

* * *

My dream of becoming a Mummy Concierge started to nudge at me again once I was newly pregnant. The moment it all made sense to me was mid mini-breakdown in the middle of a department store at three months pregnant, whilst clutching a Ewan The Dream Sheep toy and exclaiming loudly, 'Will this make me a better mummy if I buy this?'

I had excitedly bounded down the King's Road in Chelsea, shopping list in hand, ready to buy all of the baby essentials that I had spent hours researching. Four hours later, I was standing in the middle of the department store, surrounded by buggies, sleeping bags, bottles and sterilisers, manically chanting, 'I must have this, and this . . . the baby needs it.'

It wasn't my most glamorous moment.

Later that evening and back at home, a cup of tea perched on my blossoming bump like a makeshift table, my husband questioned what had happened earlier. It appears that a sales assistant had managed to relieve me of my mobile phone and tapped away a message to my husband: 'I think your wife needs you. 4th floor Peter Jones. NOW.'

Patrick had, on receipt of that text, bounded up the escalators 40 minutes later, panting and sweating, convinced something awful had happened. Instead, he found me calmly chatting to a fellow pregnant woman about perineal tears and the pros and cons of water births versus natural labour. When he took me to one side and asked what was so wrong, he had to be summoned from his work at 11am on a Tuesday morning, I calmly showed him two breast pumps and asked which one he thought would be more comfortable for breastfeeding.

There was no doubt about it: I had lost the plot . . .

But let me assure you, I was not the only pregnant woman to feel this way. Ask anyone rocking a bump about how prepared they are for becoming parents and you will see the fear flicker in their eyes. There's a desperate look that pregnant women get, the fleeting, 'Oh my fucking God, what am I doing and how do I do it?' sideways glance that confirmed to me everything I needed to know.

Pregnant women needed help – and I was going to be the one to make it happen.

PART TWO

FIRST TRIMESTER

Chapter 4

Setting up the business is probably one of the hardest things I have ever done. I spent hours at a time on Google, lengthy lists were made and numerous conversations all started with the sentence 'You're going to do WHAT?' between friends and family. The hardest part for me was actually coming up with a name for what I wanted to do. One Wednesday evening, glass of wine in hand, I sat down at my kitchen table whilst Patrick cooked supper, and started writing down options. Three hours later and I was still going – the list had grown to 42 potential business names – and my head was in my hands. I'm actually quite a creative type so enjoy this sort of brainstorming a lot, but I'm also a perfectionist and the right name for the business just wasn't coming to me. So, in a moment of exasperation, I turned to my husband (as a side note, he is certainly NOT the creative type so I didn't think for one moment he would actually be able to help). He tilted his head to one side, stirred the spaghetti he was making on the aga and then quite simply said, 'The Mummy Concierge?'

I must admit, I was blown away. The name worked perfectly: it was approachable, described exactly what my role in the business was and also meant I could create an amazing brand around it. I didn't sleep that night – I was so excited by the new name and all of the possibilities that went with it (what my website would look like, what my tagline could be, what images I needed to shoot to illustrate what I was doing) that by 5am the following morning, I had an entire A4 notebook filled with ideas – essentially the blueprint to my business and something I still treasure to this day.

Designing my business website was tough – I'm not a website designer at all – but to save costs, I decided to give it a go and having been pointed in the right direction by entrepreneurial friends, I managed to upload and design it. Next, I had to get the word out about who I was and what I was doing. Thankfully, my past career as a journalist helped a lot and I contacted people I had worked with in the past – who now worked on parenting magazines – and told them about my new venture. The press coverage was insane – I think the fact that what I was doing was so unique and that I was actually the only person in the UK doing it piqued interest – and before I knew it, I had a double-page spread in a national newspaper, was being talked about in the news and emails started pinging into my inbox from mummies needing help.

The Mummy Concierge was well on its way to turning into a successful business.

Looking back, I have no idea how I actually managed to set up a business and survive the first trimester at the same time. I think a second nature must have kicked in where I was determined to survive what could be described as a pretty terrible first trimester by distracting myself from it as much as possible. It makes me laugh when I think back to those moments when I was sitting happily in front of my laptop, designing my website and getting excited about my plans for The Mummy Concierge and then next thing I knew I'd be dashing to the bathroom to be violently sick before gargling some mouthwash and getting back to work.

One day, when morning sickness had completely crippled me, I was determined to head to a meeting I had arranged with a prestigious baby clothing brand in central London. Whether it was the rocking motion of the tube or the stifling hot weather that made it hard to breathe whilst 400 feet underground, before too long I was dramatically throwing up into my Mulberry handbag and cursing morning sickness out loud for everyone to hear.

A woman who had been sitting opposite me when my sickness episode happened kindly moved over to sit next to me and held my hair out of my face until I had emptied the entire contents of my stomach. She then took out a piece of paper, scribbled something on it, handed it to me and without saying a word, got off at the next stop. With sweat dripping into my eyes and down my neck, I fanned myself with the piece of paper before I felt able to read what was on it.

There were two words: *Sea Bands*.

As soon as I bolted out of the doors at Bond Street tube (fresh air at last!), I got out my phone and googled those two words. I had an idea of what a sea band was but no idea if it worked for morning sickness, so standing stock-still in central London, whilst everyone else buzzed and zoomed around me, I researched as much as possible before promptly pressing 'buy' on my order.

When I eventually arrived at the beautiful children's clothing store a few minutes later to meet with the owner, I relayed my tube story and, amidst fits of giggles (why do people find public nausea so funny?), she turned to me and said, 'Seriously though, the thing that saved me when I was pregnant with my first was apple cider vinegar.' She watched as I gently stroked a cashmere baby grow that she had passed my way. 'And my friend swore that her electric toothbrush always made her sickness worse, so store that away if you have one!'

As the day progressed, I became addicted to the search bar on my phone. As I moved from meeting to meeting, I searched for every known morning sickness cure out there – from the normal suggestions (ginger biscuits) to the more bizarre (heave spritz, a spray for your pulse points whenever you feel nauseous). It was only when I returned home that evening and was sorting through pre-natal vitamins (some brands can make you feel sicker than others, apparently!) that I noticed my notebook was filled with over four pages of potential morning sickness relief options. When I say I had done my research, my goodness did I mean it! My notes included tips from African tribes, tips that were used in the 1920s, science-approved cures, homeopathic cures, machines that can help with sickness, tablets, drinks, foods, feng shui . . . Honestly, if there was someone who knew everything possible about morning sickness, then that someone was me.

Heading back over towards my newly designed website, I hit the edit button and added another 'skill' to my packages.

'The First Trimester – helping you navigate everything the world throws (up) at you in the first three months, morning sickness tips included'.

13 things about the first trimester that nobody tells you

1. **You *will* stand in front of the mirror naked** and try to guess what you will look like when you're nine months pregnant. You may even get a pillow and shove it under your dress to complete the picture. However, those pregnancy hormones are going to come into play here too and you'll undoubtedly turn into an emotional wreck whilst you try to decide if you love or hate your pregnant body.

2. **You *will* become a hermit.** The thing with getting pregnant is that for the first couple of months, you're likely to keep it to yourself. This means that when friends call you up suggesting a boozy night out, you have to find an excuse not to go. Teamed with pregnancy tiredness, you will probably find that the thought of going outside seems far less appealing than snuggling up in your PJs and watching a good box set.

3. **Your online shopping orders will become uncontrollable.** As if a girl needs an excuse to shop! But when you are pregnant and can't sleep due to the nerves/excitement of that little baby inside of you, I can guarantee you will

turn to Amazon. You will discover pregnancy things that you never knew existed and that you will convince yourself you need IMMEDIATELY. Such as the THREE pregnancy pillows I bought, the 27 baby outfits I added to my basket and the 'C-section pants' that promised to make my tummy look like normal after the birth.

4. **You will read every pregnancy book going.** *What to Expect When You're Expecting*, *The Day-by-Day Pregnancy Book*, *How to Grow a Baby and Push It Out* . . . Hell, why not order the complete Amazon charts? Tick. Tick. Tick.

5. **Online communities will become your new obsession.** I promised I wouldn't go there but I did. The second I found out I was pregnant, I was on every 'pregnant mummy' app there was: Mumsnet, BabyCenter, 'what fruit is your baby today' . . . Seriously, it's madness but at the same time, it's strangely comforting. When you're up at 4am with morning sickness, you know there will be someone in one of your online communities who will be feeling the same – and because they are complete strangers, you don't mind talking about the more disgusting aspects of pregnancy such as constipation and wee samples.

6. **You will spend hours trying to work out how to conceal your bump.** In those first couple of weeks, you will feel

excited but also petrified about being pregnant. Everything you read will tell you that those first 12 weeks are the most 'dangerous' and it's 'safer' not to announce your pregnancy until you're past the three-month mark. (I have a completely opposing opinion to this, which you can read about later on in this book!) So, if your bump is starting to appear, you're going to want to hide it. Which means you have to find clothing that is still 'you' without looking like it's pregnancy clothing. My saviour: waterfall cardigans. Just genius.

7. **You will then hate every pregnancy piece of clothing you buy.** When you do eventually decide to start buying pregnancy clothes, you will wait in eager anticipation for the courier to deliver them. When they arrive, you will have a meltdown. The problem is: pregnancy clothes are awful. I have literally never come cross a single pregnancy wardrobe that is stylish. Apparently, if you are pregnant, all fashion sense has to go out of the window and you are destined to live in striped nautical T-shirts and elasticated pregnancy jeans.*

*The one light at the end of the tunnel? Pregnancy jeans *are* AMAZING. Amazing in that they will be the most comfortable thing you have ever worn and you may still be wearing them six months after you give birth . . .

8. **Medical advice varies hugely depending on what country you're in (and this will drive you mad!).** Did you know that the French don't sterilise? Here in the UK, we buy

every piece of sterilising equipment we can get our hands on, whereas the French simply put all baby gear in the dishwasher and have done with it. Same goes for blue cheese and wine. The French say 'oui' during pregnancy, the British say 'no'. I know what nationality I'd rather be . . .

9. **The exhaustion is unbearable.** You will literally feel as if a 20-stone man is hanging off your eyelids.

10. **You will google 'how to find out the sex of your child'** and then do every old wives' tale going, in secret, in your bedroom. After all, who wants to be caught in public dangling their wedding ring on a piece of string over their belly?

11. **You'll suddenly want to become best friends with any of your circle who are also pregnant, even if you hated them before.** It's a cold, hard fact. Once you're pregnant, you will become fascinated with everyone else who is also pregnant or who has had a baby and you will want them to be your best friend immediately. Cue lots of Instagram stalking and Facebook 'likes' under photos of their perfect family.

12. **You'll convince yourself you need EVERY baby product on the market.** Even that double breast pumping bra. I kid you not, even I fell for that one.

13. **You'll sometimes use your pregnancy as an excuse.** Don't fancy staying out late at a boring colleague's dinner party? Want to reject that invite to visit your parents-in-law? YOU NOW HAVE A VERY LEGITIMATE EXCUSE. Pull the 'morning sickness card', pretend you're 'so exhausted you need to be at home' or (the best tactic by far) just scream and shout and cry and then blame it on the pregnancy hormones. They will literally get you out of anything . . .

Chapter 5

It's not usually considered normal to walk through central London with a Mulberry handbag slung over the crook of your arm, heaving with the following items: 20 × sick bags, two cans of ginger beer, 'poo' drops (I'll explain more later), two wristbands that look like something an eighties aerobics instructor would wear, non-alcoholic red wine and a tub of peanut butter. In fact, I'm pretty certain if I was suddenly hit by a bus, the paramedics who opened my handbag and revealed the contents would add 'probably a little insane' to my death certificate.

But, once again, it's just part and parcel of my job. And today is no different. Shrugging my bag over to my other arm, I squint at the map on my iPhone and then back up at the road. Nodding decisively to myself, I march on a few more steps and then ring the doorbell of the pastel blue front door in front of me. I hear the chime echo inside the house and then a distant 'clacker clacker' of designer heels on marble making their way towards the door.

Instead of the typical 'yummy mummy' I was expecting to come face to face with, the door opens to reveal a

20-something woman, hunched forward, waving frantically with a plastic bag in front of her face. I step back, alarmed.

'Sorry, sorry . . . I warned you my morning sickness was bad. I can't seem to go anywhere without this.' She gestures towards the plastic bag, which I suddenly realise must be a makeshift 'sick bag' and then ushers me into her home.

I don't have time to take in my surroundings as I'm far too concerned about my latest client. Her pallor is pale with a greenish tinge and she looks as though she hasn't slept in weeks. Her hair is tied up in what suspiciously looks like a pair of knickers and every time she begins to talk, she claps her hands over her mouth and starts retching. Despite not yet being formally introduced, I feel a real sense of compassion for her – this is one newly pregnant lady who is really suffering and I need to help her.

Carefully taking her hand amidst the fear she might be about to collapse on me, I lead her down the marble corridor and into what must be her living room. The room is bathed in light, thanks to two huge sash windows looking out onto a small but immaculate garden. The whole room, I notice, is completely pristine. There is a huge white L-shaped sofa to the far right, which sits in front of a marble coffee table, currently adorned with the biggest bunch of peonies I have ever seen.

Acqua di Parma candles burn brightly (and smell gorgeous) on a small coffee table next to some beautiful-looking books all about fashion. A Brora throw in a pale, creamy green lies elegantly across a winged armchair and behind it stands an Art Deco gilded mirror, which is the size of the entire wall. The room is – without a doubt – absolutely stunning.

Placing my newest client – who has now formally introduced herself as Lucy – down onto the armchair, I find the kitchen and pour out a glass of water from the tap. Halfway, I stop myself – would this client drink tap water? – and toss it to one side whilst opening the fridge and taking out a bottle of sparkling Perrier water.

I walk back into the living room and hand over the glass, which Lucy accepts gratefully. She has composed herself a bit and a slight hint of colour has come back into her face, I notice.

'I'm so sorry about that.' She raises her eyebrows and smiles warmly before clinking her water glass against mine softly. 'You just didn't see me at my best. Goodness, who knew morning sickness could be so awful!'

We chat easily for the next 20 minutes and she tells me about her pregnancy so far, how it was all a bit of a shock (a happy one!) when she took a test and realised she was pregnant.

'My own mother was flabbergasted when I told her I was pregnant,' she explains. 'The first thing she asked was, "How could you possibly be pregnant – you don't even have a boyfriend?!"' She chuckles at the memory. 'Let's just say, I don't think *Mummy dear* has warmed to the concept that successful career women might not have time for a relationship but are happy to indulge in a casual fling every now and again!'

Lucy is single by choice (I can't imagine she's the type who ever has a problem attracting men) and became pregnant after a one-night stand with a 'gorgeously handsome Italian called Anton'.

'It was never going to be anything more than a one-night thing, just a bit of fun really!' She throws back her glossy auburn mane and laughs loudly. 'And now look at me – single and pregnant!'

I can immediately tell that this doesn't faze her. From our first chat on the phone a week ago, Lucy has given me the lowdown on her life. She's an interior designer who runs her own business (hence the beautiful house) and is completely content being fun, free and fabulous. This baby might not have been planned but she has embraced it like she does everything else in her life – with passion and excitement (and a shopping habit that has gone through the roof, thanks to all the baby paraphernalia that she now desperately 'needs').

She gets up to show me some of the bits she has bought (despite only being eight weeks pregnant) and I watch as the colour drains from her face again.

'Sorry, I think I'm going to be—'

I grab the nearest thing I can find – a decorative OKA bowl full of potpourri – and she swiftly throws up into it.

'Oh, I'm so embarrassed! Please forgive me.' She waves a hand in front of her face apologetically. 'It's this sickness, I just can't shake it.'

Handing her a tissue and disposing of the bowl in the nearest bathroom, I wait until she is ready to continue. When she is, I reach into my handbag and we set to work. After all, my job today is to do whatever I can to help make Lucy's morning sickness as bearable as possible.

'Right, so number one on the agenda is how to deal with morning sickness. Here' – I gesture towards my bag and she eyes it greedily – 'is my bag of tricks.' One by one, I take each item out and line it up on the coffee table in front of us.

For those of you reading this who have suffered with morning sickness, you will understand just how crippling it can be. Why, oh why, it's just called 'morning sickness' always astounds me. I want to re-christen it 'Any time of the day or night sickness' – it's far more apt. I've seen mothers who literally cannot leave their bed due to constant vomiting. I've dealt with mothers who are so nervous about being sick, they don't even want to leave the house. I've had mothers who take it in their stride and are very relaxed about vomiting behind a tree in a park. Some don't suffer at all and some feel nauseous but are never actually sick.

Having also suffered with morning sickness myself, I really understand the anxiety that can be all-encompassing when it comes to social situations. In the first 12 weeks of my pregnancy, I avoided any social gathering like the plague. I was, and I'm not ashamed to admit it, a social recluse. Partly because the last thing I wanted was to turn up to a party and throw up all over a new dress, and partly because in those first few months you're likely to be hiding your pregnancy from others and with constant nausea and a Diet Coke, friends at parties are likely to become suspicious.

Which is why Lucy has booked in a consultation with me to create a master plan around her morning sickness.

'Ginger tablets.' Sounding a bit like an army sergeant, I point to the orange pastilles on the coffee table. 'You need to have these with you at all times. Put a pack of them in every handbag you own so that you're never caught short.'

I have brought along a little make-up bag (another part of my morning sickness kit) and place the box of pastilles inside.

'Next, you'll need to start wearing these.' I laugh at the horrified look on Lucy's face as I produce a pair of seasickness bracelets. Easily bought online, these are the one piece of equipment I swear every pregnant mummy should own. They were first brought to my attention by that kind woman on the tube who wrote their name on a piece of paper, and I had since come across a YouTube channel of a Navy SEAL Officer giving tips on seasickness. His stocky demeanour and thick American accent told me what I needed to know – 'seasickness bands work', so I immediately ordered them and within minutes of wearing them, my morning sickness had disappeared.

I explain this to Lucy.

'But they're so ugly.' She frowns, slipping the elasticated fuzzy purple material on over her wrists. 'I literally look like I'm about to go to an eighties fancy dress party – all I need now is a fluorescent tutu and some leg warmers.'

I smile at the horrified look on her face but remind her that, as it's currently November, she should be able to cover them up with one of her gorgeous cashmere sweaters. That seems to placate her and she keeps them on throughout the rest of our consultation.

'You're going to need a lot of these,' I explain, producing about 20 aeroplane sick bags from my bag of tricks. I can see the fear flicker across her face – I presume she thinks this is my way of telling her that she's going to be being very sick for a long time yet, but this isn't what I'm getting at.

'I sometimes find that the fear of being sick – and maybe throwing up in a taxi or in the middle of the road – is something that makes mums really anxious. I always tell my clients to have a couple of sick bags in their handbags just in case. It's not because I think they will actually use them, but knowing that you have somewhere to be sick – that won't leak or stain your Mulberry – can be quite comforting,' I explain.

Relieved, Lucy grins and watches as I fold them up into the make-up bag.

I slowly take her through the next couple of items on my list – a citrus aromatherapy stick which can be rubbed onto temples and pulse points to relieve nausea, a pack of chewing gum (to get rid of the taste afterwards), a packet of almonds (snacking regularly can help keep sickness at bay) and peppermint hand cream (the smell can help relieve sickness). She balks as I show her the 'poo drops'.

'Don't worry, these are just great for disguising the smell of vomit if you end up throwing up in somebody else's bathroom!'

She takes the little bottle from me and reads the ingredients, nodding her head in interest.

'And finally . . .' I pick up everything on the table and adding it to the make-up bag, and look up at Lucy. 'What antenatal vitamins are you on?' She gets up and heads to her bedroom, before reappearing a few minutes later and handing me a brand of vitamins specifically aimed at pregnant women. They are the type that have all the vitamins you need in one vitamin tablet. I frown down at them.

'This could be your problem,' I explain, turning the packet over in my hands. 'Some women find that when they take these sorts of vitamin, it actually makes them feel sick. Obviously, it's always a good idea to check with your doctor first, but from personal experience, you might be better off just buying individual folic acid tablets and vitamin D tablets rather than these multivitamins. It's a tip a midwife told me and it's worked for many of my mummies.'

I hand Lucy the little make-up bag with a smile. 'Here's your morning sickness SOS kit.' I tap it against her knee. 'Now, let's raise a glass of Perrier to feeling better soon.'

We clink glasses and I see the look of relief pass over her face.

Right, one client down, one more to go . . .

*   *   *

Looking at my watch, I realise my meeting with Lucy has gone on longer than I expected, so I rush down the steps to the Underground and jump on the tube heading towards Canary Wharf. I'm due to meet another client who is also just few weeks pregnant – although her request is a little more 'wacky'.

Forty minutes later, I step out onto the concourse at Canary Wharf and run over towards Jane, who is tapping away urgently on her BlackBerry. I have met her numerous times before as we worked together when she first started her fertility treatment a few months ago. Thankfully, this meeting is not like one of our past meetings – where I would console her over the IVF not working and we would look into other fertility doctors. This time, she is pregnant – nine weeks and counting – and I'm here to help her out with something that I can only describe as interesting.

'You're here!' She throws her arms around me and stands up straight in front of me, sucking in her tummy. 'You can't tell, can you?'

I raise an eyebrow at her in amusement and shake my head. 'You look incredible. And no – no one will know. Shall we make a move?'

Jane is a very big deal in the city. So much so that she is one of the highest regarded (and probably highest paid) women in the investment bank where she works. Having spent her twenties and thirties working her way up the career ladder, thoughts of becoming a mother only began to appear when she turned 40. Three years of numerous unsuccessful attempts at IVF and she had been ready to throw in the towel, until only a few weeks ago when a miracle happened and the pregnancy test turned positive.

But there was a problem. Like so many women, Jane was apprehensive about telling her work too soon about her pregnancy. Understandably, she was nervous. It was still early days and after such a horrific couple of years trying to conceive, she was very cautious about something going wrong and losing the baby. She also knew that being pregnant and telling your boss can be daunting and worrying. So, for the time being, she wants to keep it a secret. And that's why I'm here.

'The party started an hour ago, so they are all probably already two sheets to the wind,' she explains as we walk past a gaggle of girls in their twenties retouching their make-up and head over to the bar. Jane has just been promoted (another reason she is nervous about announcing her pregnancy) and, as such, her team have decided to throw her a party.

'And with a party comes drinks . . . alcoholic ones,' she explains. 'And I'll be expected to drink them.'

We had brainstormed ideas about how she could get around this a week beforehand, but everything had been met with resistance:

'I can't say I'm hungover and that's why I'm not drinking because it's unprofessional to turn up hungover at work.'

'Nope, can't say I'm on antibiotics. One of my colleagues' wives is a doctor and she's bound to start questioning me.'

'Ha! If I just say I'm not drinking, it will raise too many suspicions. That's the last thing I want.'

In the end, we decided that the only thing that would work is for Jane to have a 'wingwoman' – and that wingwoman was to be me.

I can see an area that has been cordoned off and raucous bellows and laughs are coming from it. Someone immediately spots Jane and waves a bottle of champagne in her direction.

'Here she is! The Woman of the Moment! Let's get you a glass of bubbles . . .'

Jane and I exchange glances and I subtly give her a nod of encouragement.

'Oh, I actually really fancy a G and T first,' she explains, hugging the champagne bearer and kissing another man on the cheek in greeting. 'Long day – I think gin is the only thing to fix it.'

This is my cue. I quickly introduce myself as Jane's friend to her group of co-workers, then say loudly, 'Jane, I'm heading to the bar. I'll get you that G and T.' She smiles at me gratefully and I can see her shoulders relax.

We can do this.

Ten minutes later, I return to find her chatting animatedly to some of her female colleagues and I pass her a glass filled with tonic and ice and garnished with a wedge of lemon.

'Your G and T,' I say loudly, so everyone can hear.

The rest of the night passes in much the same way. When someone hands Jane a glass of champagne, she takes 'pretend' sips and then places it on a table, where I exchange it for a glass of sparkling water. Everyone else at the party has had their fair share of alcohol and they're far too tipsy to notice that she's sipping on water, not Cristal.

In the taxi home later that evening, Jane – who has taken off her heels and is rubbing her swollen feet – exhales slowly. 'Thank you, Tiffany,' she says. 'I can't quite believe we pulled that off.'

'My pleasure,' I respond, stifling a yawn and smiling to myself.

Who would ever have thought that one of my 'jobs' as a Mummy Concierge would be swapping champagne for water? Watching the lights of London whizz past, I feel a swell of pride in my stomach. For some, tonight might have seemed like a bit of a gimmick, but for Jane it was exactly what she needed. I take out my notebook and cross off the items on my to-do list with satisfaction.

1. Morning sickness SOS bag ✓
2. Disguising early pregnancy ✓

Not a bad day's work at all.

Chapter 6

It's not often I merge work with my own personal life, but in this situation, it seemed silly not to.

I was two months pregnant and one of my clients, Kathryn (who had discovered me after reading an article in the newspaper about my job), was also pregnant and due at around the same time. She had contacted me initially via an email that was so long, I had to sit down with a hot cup of tea (which was finished before I even finished reading the email). Like any first-time mother, she was mostly obsessed with the birth and had explained in detail in her email her worries and concerns about how she was going to give birth. Like me, Kathryn was going to have her baby privately, but didn't know which hospital or which obstetrician to go with.

It was on our first phone call that she suggested a 'birth-date'.

'Oh, it will be hysterical! You're pregnant, I'm pregnant, let's do the hospital tours together! My husband doesn't care where I give birth so long as the food is good, so it would be nice to have another pregnant woman's opinion.'

I could hear her smiling down the phone. My initial reaction was to say no. I was quite looking forward to

Patrick being with me (and felt it was important) when we met obstetricians, but when I explained this to him, he quickly encouraged me to take Kathryn up on her offer.

'Look, you know you don't want to give birth in a birthing pool.' He laughed as I visibly shuddered at the thought. 'But it might be good for you to see it and to learn how other forms of birth work at each hospital so that you can feed back to any new clients.'

Goodness, he was so right.

'You look around the hospitals with her and then we can try and make appointments for the same afternoon to meet one of the obstetricians – and I'll come with you.'

* * *

Two weeks later, I was following Kathryn and a buxom midwife through a labyrinth of corridors at Queen Charlotte's and Chelsea Hospital in west London.

'So, you're wanting a C-section?' The midwife pulled her half-moon glasses down her nose and looked over at me expectantly. 'That would take place in here. This is one of our many operating theatres.'

I poked my head around the door to see a sterile-looking room complete with an operating table, various bits of equipment and bright lights.

Yup, that would do me fine.

I must admit, when I first found out I was pregnant, I did spend a lot of time agonising over how I would give birth.

Deep down, I knew I wanted a C-section – this seemed much less scary to me than having a baby via your vagina – but I still felt the need to justify my decision to myself and anyone else who asked. I vividly recall lying in a bath and writing a list of 'pros and cons' of every birth option. The list took me so long to write, by the time I was finished the bath water had gone cold and I was actually shivering.

In the end, the decision was easy. I was never going to opt for a water birth (I didn't like lukewarm baths at the best of times, let alone when trying to push a small human out of my body) and I wasn't brave enough to try having my baby naturally (even the thought of it made me tense up, which I presumed wouldn't be good when it came to the actual delivery). There was something about having a scheduled C-section and knowing the exact date and time your baby would arrive that made me feel calm. I suppose that just shows how much of a control freak I am! Once the decision had been made, I didn't worry so much about the technicalities around it. If I was going to have a C-section, then it would be in an operating theatre – and most operating theatres looked pretty much the same.

Beside me, Kathryn shuddered. 'I can't believe you want to be cut open,' she whispered, clutching my hand as she did so. I could tell she was nervous – we both were. Looking around hospitals and seeing the place where your baby might enter the world is rather mind-blowing and nerve-racking at the same time.

'And this is one of our birthing rooms . . .' The midwife swung open the door to a room which looked like it belonged in a children's nursery. The walls were hand-painted with images of beaches, whales and dolphins and I could hear some sort of 'warbling' coming from the speakers.

'It's whale music,' the midwife explained, clocking my look of confusion. 'Some of the mothers find it relaxes them and enables them to get into the "zone".' Kathryn and I had bonded hugely during this hospital tour and so I nudged her playfully in the ribs, expecting her to join me in thinking about the absurdness of this birthing suite. But when I looked over at her, I saw she was staring in wonder at the room, her hands clasped to her cheeks in amazement.

'Oh my goodness, I HAVE to have my baby here!' she squealed and actually jumped up and down on the spot. 'This is just incredible. The music, the murals . . . I can't think of a better place for my baby to enter the world than this.'

Whilst I stepped back in shock – *surely she was joking?* – the midwife took Kathyryn's hand and led her over to what can only be described as a big paddling pool in the middle of the room.

'This is the birthing pool.'

Kathryn stood by the pool and breathed in and out deeply. *Was it me or was she actually practising her 'labour breathing' now?*

'And this' – the midwife handed her what looked like a small TV remote – 'controls the lights in the room so that they match your mood.'

Kathryn pressed one of the small buttons and the room was flooded in a purple haze. I watched as she prodded a different bottom and the room changed from purple to pink to blue.

'This is just so relaxing, don't you think?'

I realised she was talking to me and so I tried to pull myself out of my stupor.

* * *

Later that afternoon, Kathryn and I finished our hospital tour with a debrief in the quaint little café opposite.

'Do you ever worry people will judge you for having a C-section?' Kathryn was contemplatively sucking on the straw of her pink smoothie. I was about to protest, but she continued, 'I know that if I have a water birth, people will think I'm a warrior and that's pretty important to me.'

I coughed on my tea and tried to regain my composure.

Surely she couldn't be choosing a birth option because she was worried about what people would think of her?

Before I knew it, hot angry tears were running down Kathryn's face. I reached for a napkin and handed it to her hurriedly so she could dab at her tears.

'All my friends have had water births or natural births without any pain relief. They all gave each other cards with "warrior" written on them. They always talk about how the way you give birth defines you as a woman and I don't want to be the one who isn't deserving of the warrior title.'

I must have look horrified as Kathryn then burst into fits of laugher whilst simultaneously wiping away tears. 'I know. Mad, eh? But I just feel like if I don't try a natural birth, I'll be judged forever. And anyway, they all did it, so I guess I must be able to do it too.' Her eyes misted over and I noticed that the hand gripping her smoothie was shaking. 'The thing is, I'm scared. All I really want is an epidural or a C-section like you, but I feel like it's not an option for me.'

'What about your reactions in the hospital?' I was referring to her initial excitement when we saw the birthing room.

'I suppose I'm trying to convince myself.' A solitary tear rolled down her cheek.

This wasn't the last time I had this conversation. In the years to come, working as a Mummy Concierge, I have had countless mummies-to-be fall apart on me due to the pressure to have 'the perfect birth'. Only last year (2020), I worked with a mother who had been convinced by friends and family to have a 'natural' birth. She sent me a text on the day her baby was born and instead of words filled with excitement and wonder at becoming a new mummy, I could practically hear the tears through the text she sent: 'I'm lying in intensive care feeling drained. I lost 3.5 litres of blood during delivery and my little boy is now in an entirely different ward to me because I ended up in intensive care. Why did I let myself be bullied into having this sort of birth?'

It's true that there is an invisible birth story hierarchy. I've noticed it mostly with new mothers I meet at the nursery or soft play. There is definitely a sense of pride if a mother has had a completely natural, no 'pain relief' birth. Also, the longer the birth goes on for, and the more horrific it is, the bigger your badge of honour gets. It's one of the first questions other mums will ask after you've had a baby: what sort of a birth did you have? Complete strangers will quite willingly ask how you birthed your baby. I vividly recall the feeling of inadequacy when I admitted to my NCT class that I was having a C-section. Twelve pairs of eyes looked back at me with a lack of respect and I could almost hear the whispers of, 'She's taking the easy route, she's not having her baby properly.' I honestly felt I had failed, even before I actually became a mother. Thankfully, I have now come to terms with how I gave birth – my body, my choice. I find the judgement women put on their peers about how they gave birth horrifying. Childbirth isn't a joke, no one considers getting root canal done without anaesthetic, so why would pain relief while pushing another human being out of you be any different and who is anyone to judge you for that?

Becoming a mother is tough enough – you have to adapt to a new role that no one has trained you to do and you suddenly, literally, have someone else's life in your hands. You then have to run the gauntlet of being judged on the methods by which your child arrived. Does it make us lesser human beings if we choose to have pain relief to help with the safe arrival of our baby? And why do some women feel the need to shout about it on their Instagram stories that they did it the 'natural' way and didn't 'give in' by opting for pain relief? It's moments like this when I want to wave a brightly coloured flag, stand on a table and shout, 'Giving birth is not a competition!'

'Listen to me.' I took Kathryn's chin in my hand and forced her to look at me. 'There is no failure to be found in any person brave enough to go through the process of childbirth, no matter what that process may be. You do you. Listen . . .' I raised my voice slightly to make sure she heard every word. 'You. Do. You,' I repeated.

It's a motto I would repeat over and over again through-out the next few years. I said it to the mummy who was scared about not breastfeeding her baby, the mother who wanted to co-sleep but was being shamed for doing it by her friends, the new mum who let her baby sleep in the same room until they were two and the mother who moved their baby into the nursery at ten days old.

In the end, Kathryn decided she wanted to go back to the hospital and talk to the midwife fully about all birthing options.

'Thank you,' she said as she walked back towards the hospital building. 'I needed that pep talk.' She slung her handbag over her shoulder defiantly and for the first time that day I saw a genuine smile on her face.

'You do you.'

She laughed and shook her head in acceptance. 'I think I may have to have that as my life motto now. Just make sure you live by it too!' She winked mischievously in my direction and I laughed back. She must have remembered that first chat we had where I confided to her the pressure I felt to 'babywear' when my baby was born.

'Who needs a baby sling when you can get a top-of-the-range pushchair!' she yelled, before disappearing through the hospital revolving doors. 'You DO you!'

* * *

Meeting the person who might deliver your baby can be an interesting experience. Patrick had arrived at our hospital and we were heading off to meet Dr John, an obstetrician strongly recommended to us by a friend of ours. 'He's a complete character,' she explained at a dinner party the week before. 'You'll just love him. He delivered both of our babies and I'd have another just so he could do it again.'

Her enthusiasm had filled both Patrick and I with confidence and so we booked an initial meeting with him as soon as we could. The hospital he worked from was not one I had visited before, but like many hospitals in London, it seemed fully equipped with the latest gadgets and we were offered a plethora of biscuits, teas and coffees by his PA. The PA had explained on the phone at the time of booking that Dr John would be thrilled to do an initial scan for us, just to confirm everything was going well and that there was indeed a baby in there.

On entering his office, a stocky man with bright blond hair combed to one side greeted us, but instead of the usual, 'Welcome, I'm your doctor, pleased to meet you,' I was met with the following: 'Right, let's get your knickers off and do this scan.' I must have looked shocked (and probably nervous), but his next sentence didn't offer much comfort either: 'Don't be nervous. If I'm going to deliver your baby, I'm probably going to see you poo yourself during birth so we might as well get acquainted now.'

Let's just say, Patrick and I didn't stick around for the scan. On reflection, there is one thing I have learnt about the people you surround yourself with during pregnancy and birth – you need to find 'your tribe' – the types that speak the same language as you, understand your worries and concerns, and know how to put you at ease.

'Oh, he said the same to me when I met him.' My friend laughed when I regaled her with the story about her top-notch obstetrician. 'I thought it was hysterical and he immediately put me at ease – that's why I love him.'

That day, I concluded having a baby really is an 'each to their own' thing. And one thing I had learnt was that what works for one pregnant mummy-to-be might not work for another.

PART THREE

SECOND TRIMESTER

Chapter 7

I remember the first time I was interviewed on the radio about my job as a Mummy Concierge and being a nervous wreck. I had hormones racing around my body at a rate of knots, I spent my days floating on air at the prospect that my baby was going to arrive or cursing pregnancy and the hot sweats/aching feet. However, I was determined to pull myself together for this interview (a lot of clients had excitedly texted me that morning saying they were going to tune in so I didn't want to let anyone down).

Patrick and I arrived at the radio station's studio in central Oxford and were told to wait in the reception area until my name was called. Every couple of minutes I excused myself to go to the loo, where I swiftly wiped off and then reapplied the red lipstick I was wearing. It was only after my third trip in as many minutes that he reminded me, 'You're doing a RADIO segment, Tiff. No one is actually going to SEE you.' Fair play to him – I guess those hours poring over the make-up counter in Harvey Nicks two days beforehand really weren't worth the effort.

I had been contacted a few days earlier as they had read a piece in the newspaper about my job as a Mummy Concierge and thought it sounded intriguing. It was my first 'Mummy Concierge' radio interview with the press and I couldn't wait to talk about how the business had started and developed over the last couple of months. As anyone who has set up their own business knows, getting the word out there is one of the hardest parts, so I was hugely excited about going live on air and letting people know that I existed. However, everything took a slightly surreal turn when the producer for the show suddenly noticed my baby bulge protruding from my sweater and said, 'Were you trying for a baby?'

I can see where his good intentions were coming from (a lot of men in particular see a pregnant woman and feel that they have to comment) but when I was pregnant, I spent the entire nine months dodging personal questions and unwanted advice about having a baby as much as possible. It's amazing how, as soon as you announce you are pregnant, people seem to want to impart their words of wisdom on you (regardless of whether or not they have actually been pregnant/parented a child themselves). People also feel it's completely acceptable to ask details about your body, where you conceived your baby and so on, regardless of the fact they are just standing next to you in a line in Starbucks. I suppose you could say it's one of my bugbears, which is completely ridiculous really, seeing as my job as a Mummy Concierge is to do exactly that – give out advice! Let's just say, whenever I meet with my clients, I'm careful to read through my list of what not to say to a pregnant woman that I had made when I was pregnant – just to be sure I don't get off on the wrong foot!

What not to say to a pregnant woman

1. **'Were you trying for a baby?'** No, we were trying for a hippopotamus.

2. **'Ooh, did I just see your baby *move*?'** I kid you not, this was said to me whilst sitting in a coffee shop with some friends from my NCT class. I was seven-and-a-bit months pregnant and a complete stranger came up to me and said that exact line. Not only did I find it incredibly strange she had found the need to stare at my stomach for an elongated amount of time, but also, NO, THE BABY WASN'T MOVING! I was probably just breathing. It's funny how your stomach moves when you breathe, isn't it?

3. **'Make sure you sleep whilst you can because once the baby arrives, you won't be able to.'** Oh yes, this little gem of wisdom. Because it's so easy to sleep when there's another person inhabiting your body, kicking your bladder and squishing your stomach so you have indigestion and heartburn.

4. **'Have you worked out when the baby was conceived?'** Yes, I have actually. Would you like me to tell you the details? Yes? OK, well, it was doggy style in the back of

my husband's car whilst we were delayed getting to my best friend's wedding.* See? Did you REALLY want to know?

*Please note our baby was NOT conceived in this way. And yes, I do know where and when, but I will not be telling you.

5. **'OMG, I have to tell you about my super-traumatic birth!'** No, nope, *never*! No pregnant woman ever needs to hear your horror stories.

6. **'Are you sure it's OK to eat/drink that?'** Unless you're a doctor, don't ask a pregnant woman this. Trust me, we've already looked up how much caffeine we're allowed to have in a day and we know we can't eat blue cheese, rare meat, drink booze . . . Although you might think of it as 'helping', having everyone around you police your food and beverage intake can be rather annoying. (One client of mine was accosted by a fellow customer in line at the supermarket, who said, 'You know you're not allowed to drink, right?' Yes, but last time we checked, pregnant women were still able to buy a bottle of wine for others.)

7. **'I can't imagine you being a mummy to a boy.'** Why would anyone need to hear that you think they'll be a terrible mother to a specific gender?

8. **'You don't actually look pregnant from behind.'** Yes, that's because my uterus is in the front.

9. **'You are MASSIVE. Honestly, you're as big as a house!'** Just ask yourself how many people you know who would be pleased to be compared to a massive house. None. So please don't say it to a pregnant woman.

10. **'Can I touch your belly?'** Let me put a spin on this for you. If someone came up to you and said, 'Can I lick your arm?' or 'Would I be able to poke your elbow?', you'd probably find it a bit strange, right? So why do people feel that it's perfectly OK, now that you're pregnant, to start touching parts of your body they would NEVER have touched before? MOVE AWAY FROM THE BUMP!

11. **'Are you really sure you want a C-section/water birth/ no pain relief? Have you *really* thought about it?'** Nope, I just picked the idea out of a great big hat and decided to go with it. OF COURSE, I'VE BLOODY THOUGHT ABOUT IT! It's not a decision you just pick out of the blue.

Chapter 8

From the day I found out I was pregnant, I was convinced I was having a little girl. Lots of people say 'a mother just knows' and I agree with this wholeheartedly. There was something – call it the bond with my unborn child – that just felt it could sense a girl. As far as I was concerned, I was 100 per cent carrying a mini-me.

Too impatient to wait until I gave birth, we decided to pay for the harmony test – a blood test and scan that you can pay for privately that not only checks the health of your baby but also tells you the gender with 99 per cent accuracy. It was late December and we shivered our way down Harley Street – scarves pulled up around our faces, hats pulled down over our foreheads to keep out the cold. I was a bundle of nerves as the test also analyses DNA from the foetus which circulates in the mother's blood and can tell you if your child is at risk from abnormalities and cognitive heart defects. Although we knew we wouldn't get the results immediately, it still played on my mind that this test would tell us how healthy our baby was.

As the sonographer rubbed the warm jelly on my tummy and started looking at her screen, I could feel my body tense.

Please let my baby be OK. I don't care what gender he or she is, just so long as they're OK.

A week later, we had a call from the clinic, reassuring us that our baby was fine and asking if we'd like to know the gender. I asked if they were able to email our obstetrician, Natasha, with the news instead. We were seeing her the next day and Patrick and I had a plan.

The following day, we arrived at The Kensington Wing in Chelsea and, clutching a small package, headed into Natasha's room for our appointment. At first, I was embarrassed to explain our plan.

'Natasha, we have a favour to ask you.'

She looked up from my maternity notes and smiled. 'Let me guess. Is this something to do with the gender of the baby?'

'This is probably the strangest thing you've been asked.' Blushing, I nod to Patrick, who picks up the package from the floor by his feet and hands it to Natasha.

'We've bought a pair of cashmere baby socks. They are reversible. One side is pink and one is blue.'

I could see Patrick shift slightly in his seat. I think he was embarrassed. When I'd told him my plan the evening before, he had physically balked and exclaimed that I 'couldn't ask a doctor to do that'. But I was determined – this was our baby and I wanted to make this moment as special as possible.

'I think the clinic emailed you yesterday with the results of the gender scan. So, we were wondering . . .' I stumble slightly.

Maybe we *are* asking too much from our doctor?

'You want me to turn the socks the right way round – blue for a boy and pink for a girl – and then wrap them up as a Christmas present for you?' I can hear the smile in Natasha's voice and when I look up at her, I can see she is beaming.

'You don't mind?'

'Of course I don't! And believe me, this is one of the "easier" gender reveals I've had to do!'

At this, Patrick sits up straight and leans forward – he loves stories like this. 'What's the most extravagant gender reveal you've heard of?'

For the next ten minutes we are all in hysterics. Natasha has Patrick snorting tea through his nose as she tells a story about a couple who wanted confetti cannons to be set off as they left her office. The idea was that they would be covered in pink or blue confetti in the reception of the hospital. Natasha has to explain this probably wasn't the most sensible option considering the waiting room was likely to be filled with anxious pregnant women who might not enjoy the sound of confetti cannons exploding in their ears.

'I actually had a father who emailed me recently wanting to tell his girlfriend the sex of their baby. She hadn't wanted to find out, but he did, so he emailed saying he wanted to surprise her by flying her in a helicopter for her to look out the window to see hay bales spelling out: It's a boy.' Natasha gasps and covers her mouth with her hands. 'I quickly explained to him this probably wasn't the best idea. Not only had his girlfriend specially said she DIDN'T want to find out the gender, I also didn't think it was a good idea flying an eight-and-a-half-months pregnant woman up in a small plane – what if she went into labour?'

When we leave Natasha's office, I'm holding a small package wrapped up in festive paper with a note attached.

I couldn't wait.

Since the day I found out I was pregnant, I had spun a collective daydream about our little girl: I pictured her walking through life with confidence and long, wavy hair (often tied up in a French plait with ribbons at the end). She'd be my willing partner in crime when her daddy suggested watching rugby on TV (we'd both jump on him and demand a cheesy chick flick instead). I'd take her to ballet classes when she was three and watch her twirl around in a lilac tutu and blush pink leotard. She would be the one who would demand stories about princesses at bedtime and would share my love of musicals (often found singing songs from *Les Mis* first thing in the morning in her bed).

As she grew older, I could talk to her about love, wipe away the tears when her heart was first broken and take her shopping for that first bra. We would be best friends and although her daddy could do no wrong, she would trust me implicitly and know I was a mummy who loved her with my whole entire being.

Enter, Christmas Day 2018. Patrick and I were in Ireland, spending Christmas with his family. The night before, I had unpacked all of our suitcases, carefully placing the neatly wrapped Christmas presents under the tree and laughing with my sister-in-law over whether a non-alcoholic mulled wine really was as tasty as the real thing (FYI, it's not). I had gone to bed the night before, hand on my bump, talking animatedly to Patrick about what our lives would look like this time next year.

'We'll be able to put her in a gorgeous red dress with white tights and we can put a Christmas ribbon in her hair and—'

'*She* might be a *he*,' Patrick interrupted, raising his eyebrows at me but knowing he was already defeated. Despite his insistence that he didn't care if we had a girl or boy, I think he found my assurance that we were having a girl quite baffling at times.

'I just know she's a she,' I insisted for about the millionth time that month. I would never admit to him that I had also done just about every old wives' tale in the book and they had all confirmed my instinct: the wedding ring had hung on a piece of string around my belly and had swung back and forth in a straight line, I was carrying my bump 'high', I had had terrible morning sickness, sweet cravings and spotty breakouts – all of which Google had confirmed to me meant I was a mother to a daughter.

Before switching off the light, I felt around under the bed and my hand brushed over the wrapped package that Natasha had given us a few weeks before. I honestly felt like I was three years old again – willing for Christmas morning to come as quickly as possible so that I could confirm I was going to have a daughter.

Every half-hour on Christmas Day, I had a text from my parents who were celebrating Christmas at my sister's house in London, asking if we knew yet.

'Not yet . . . just waiting for the right moment,' I typed back.

The right moment came after Christmas lunch, when everyone was full to the brim with turkey and mince pies and various members of the family were heading off on a post-Christmas lunch walk, or slumping down on the sofas to watch a Christmas movie.

Patrick looked over at me, a small grin on his face. 'Now?' he whispered.

The surge of adrenaline rocked through my body and I nodded quickly, not knowing whether to burst with excitement or be sick with nerves. He took my hand and we walked out of the kitchen and into the sitting room.

'Wait, wait, we have to record it!' I raced out of the sitting room and up to the bedroom to grab my phone, returning quickly to set it up, carefully pointing at the sofa.

'Do we have to?' Patrick grimaced as I pressed 'record'.

'Of course, we do! We can remember this moment forever and show her when she's bigger.'

The mood changed suddenly. There was a tension in the air as the reality of what we were about to reveal hit us. Quietly, Patrick turned to me again, beckoning for me to sit on the sofa next to him.

'Let's do this . . .'

In my excitement at planning the reveal, I had given Natasha swathes of blue and pink tissue paper and asked her to wrap the socks in alternating colours. It was essentially a game of adult pass the parcel – if you couldn't play a game like that on Christmas Day, then when else could you do it?

Patrick handed the parcel to me and I tore away the first layer of blue tissue. I handed it back and the next layer of pink was discarded. We carried on like this for a few more layers, each stripping off the paper, getting closer and slower as we neared the final layer.

'This is the final piece.' He nodded down towards the parcel. 'You do it. I know how important this is to you.'

So I closed my eyes and slowly began to peel away the last piece of paper. I felt the soft cashmere in my hands and cupped the socks between my fingers.

This was it! Once I opened my eyes, I would know for certain.

I pulled out a blue pair of cashmere socks and burst into tears. Patrick immediately ran over, switched off the phone that was recording our reaction and placed tight arms around me in a hug.

'Tiff, it's OK . . . A little boy is going to be amazing. We are having a little boy!'

I think it suddenly hit him and I could tell he was thrilled. But here I was, feeling the exact opposite emotion. Not knowing what to do, I ran from the room and threw myself down on the mattress in our bedroom. The tears wouldn't stop coming. I remember Patrick coming in and trying to comfort me, but I pushed him away. One thought kept running through my head: *How would I ever be able to be a good mummy to a little boy?*

* * *

'Gender disappointment' was not a term I was familiar with, but one I quickly learnt. As the tears dried, I sat up in bed and started to google. Hundreds of forums on sites like Mumsnet and the BabyCenter popped up on my screen with varying degrees of sympathy and anger.

'Can't you just be happy that you're having a baby, regardless of the sex? I've been infertile for . . .'

'Why are you moaning about having a girl? Girls are amazing. You'll love it once she is here.'

'You shouldn't be crying over the fact the baby isn't the gender you wanted, you should be more concerned that you have a healthy little boy.'

Delving further into the abyss of baby forums, I eventually found women who were feeling the same way as me: helpless and sad. Add then the main emotion – guilt – for judging their little one before they were even born. I typed out my emotions into a short post and waited for the response. They came thick and fast, and thankfully, I seemed to have found a group of mums who understood what I was feeling.

'It's absolutely fine to feel the way you are. It's easy to think that little boys will bond more with their daddy. But

I PROMISE you, the bond a little boy has with his mummy is irreplaceable.'

Everything I read was true – I was grieving for the dreams I had had about having a daughter, about how I thought we would share a special and tight bond. But now I knew we were having a boy, I found myself cringing nervously over my new vision of what life would be: video games, mud, chaos, sports. It seems stupid now, but all I could picture were the stereotypical boy characteristics. I didn't know how to be a 'boy mum' and that really scared me.

A few days passed and my internet history was streams and streams of articles on gender disappointment. But it was on a walk in the woods were things slowly started to change. It had been a hard couple of days – mainly because 1) it was Christmas and I was spoiling it for everyone by bursting into tears every couple of seconds, and 2) because I felt an intense guilt for ruining our gender reveal for Patrick. When he thought I wasn't looking, I could see him actually shine when he spoke to his mum about being a father to a little boy. I noticed he'd been looking up boys' names on his iPad and his dad had already announced he would be the first one to buy him an Irish rugby shirt.

So, fuelled by another meltdown (me, not him), Patrick suggested we take a stroll down through the woods and have a chat. We had been doing this since the start of our relationship – in true British style whenever something seems to get too much, either a cup of tea or a walk seems to pretty much solve it. I pulled my Barbour jacket on begrudgingly – it was pouring with rain (something I realised happens a lot in Ireland) and I had a feeling this 'chat' might result in more tears (if there were any left!)

We walked in silence for the first 20 minutes, me brushing away raindrops from my forehead and Patrick strolling confidently ahead, breaking off the odd dead tree branch and kicking up leaves.

'OK, so I have a plan . . . Let's think about the positives of having a boy.'

'There aren't any,' I said stubbornly, determined to remain in my depressed state. (As a side note, I know this makes me sound horribly selfish. I am very aware that having a healthy baby is all that matters, but sometimes pregnancy hormones just take control and you turn into a real nightmare!)

'Number one . . .' Patrick was resolutely ignoring me. 'Apparently little boys have incredible bonds with their mummies. My mum was saying just yesterday that the bond she had with me when I was born was indescribable. And you always mention how close the two of us are.'

I nod in agreement, but the frown remains etched on my face.

'And what about all those other things you can do with him as he gets older? I could be responsible for taking him to rugby matches, but you could take him to Ibiza!'

My eyes lit up – *now that DID sound like fun!*

'And it doesn't mean because he's a boy, he won't still love going to watch all those musicals you adore and what's to say he can't do rugby AND ballet? He might turn out to be a really thoughtful, emotional little man who loves the arts and cuddling his mummy. He might not even LIKE rugby.' Patrick smiles sideways at me as he says this and I can feel my resolve weaken.

He was right. What's to say that my little boy was going to end up like the stereotypical 'little boy' people project on us? What's to say he wouldn't just be the most fabulous, creative, intelligent, fun and happy little man ever to grace this world? Who says he can't be England's number one chef or dancer? Hell, if I was having a little girl, I'd want her to know she could be whoever she wanted to be – so why have I let a gender decide the characteristics of my little boy?

As we rounded back towards the house, I felt my mood lift and I put my hand on my pregnant belly. 'Hello, little man,' I whispered quietly, imagining my little boy snuggled up tightly in there, dreaming about who and what he would be when he entered the world. 'I can't wait to meet you.' I looked up at Patrick and he pulled me into a hug.

Suddenly everything seemed all right with the world again.

How to prepare for your baby if you don't find out the gender

- **Get neutral newborn onesies and swaddles** – Newborn babies look gorgeous in plain white baby grows, but if you want to add a bit of colour you can opt for light green or yellow onesies and swaddles. Get enough to last you a week or two and then you can buy more later in more colours if you need.

- **Create a neutral palette that can go either way** – You can still decorate your nursery without knowing the gender simply by decorating the majority of it in neutral greys or beiges until the baby comes. You can then create two Amazon wish lists which have options for added extras for both genders. Then, when your little one arrives, and you're sitting in hospital, simply click 'buy now' and you'll have all the little extras delivered to your door before you even leave the hospital.

- **Have a baby shower after the baby is born** – Instead of having a baby shower before the baby is born, have a party afterwards. That way, everyone will know the gender of your baby and can buy gifts based on the news if they want to. It also means you're more likely to get gifts you actually want, too!

- **You can buy a lot of baby kit without knowing the gender.** Spend your time buying the following: pram, cot, car seat, baby gym, baby carrier and muslins.

How to deal with gender disappointment

1. **Follow people on social media who have children of the same sex that you're about to have.** It can really help you to imagine life with your little one.

2. **Go and have another scan and, if you are allowed to, film the ultrasound.** Actually being able to see the baby and re-watch it makes you realise that you have a small human being inside you and that little person is amazing, no matter what the gender.

3. **Go shopping for boy/girl clothes.** If you wanted a little girl and have been obsessing over pretty girl dresses, then go and have a look at what boys' clothes are available. Not all of them are dinosaurs and lime green!

4. **Start designing the nursery.** One of the biggest triggers for me was when I saw images of girls' nurseries and I couldn't imagine having a little boy in a boy's nursery. But as soon as you start designing the nursery for your little man, everything becomes more real. You can begin to picture and reframe what your life is going to be like.

5. **Name your baby.** Sometimes actually having a name before the baby is born is a fabulous way of bonding. It can make you feel much more connected.

6. **Read stories from other women who have gone through gender disappointment.** Some women are so open about the gut-wrenching pain they are going through and it helps you feel less alone. Gender disappointment isn't talked about a lot because there is a fear of judgement from others.

7. **Talk to your baby.** It might feel strange at first but from around 15 weeks, your baby can actually hear your voice. If you find it hard to 'chat' to them, then look up pregnancy meditations as they are a lovely thing to do in your quiet time and can also really help you bond with your little one.

Chapter 9

'Does my vagina look OK?'

I blush, pull my shoulders back ('Act professional,' I mutter to myself) and walk over to where my client lies spreadeagled on her kitchen table.

'It's hard to tell from that angle.' I glance over as quickly as I can in the right direction and then turn my back on the pretence of finishing packing my client Juliet's hospital bag.

'It looks amazing, darling. Frank is doing to die!' Juliet's best friend Juno pronounces the word 'die' as if it's spelt 'die–ya' and I've noticed, in the last hour I've been here, that she tends to say everything with an explanation mark at the end.

She is probably the loudest woman I have ever met.

'Do you really think so? I mean, it's a fun little "before baby arrives" gift, isn't it? Might as well have evidence that it didn't used to look like a warzone pre-baby.'

Juno and Juliet laugh hysterically. 'I still can't believe you're doing a plaster cast of your vagina!' The two women break into a fit of giggles and I force myself to smile.

Why am I being so uptight? It's not as though I haven't seen a woman's vagina before.

I'd been dreading today for numerous reasons. The fact I'm eight months pregnant, feeling fat and frumpy and, quite frankly, have hormones zooming around my body at the rate of knots isn't helping. When I woke up this morning, I told Patrick what my day entailed and he laughed solidly for 20 minutes, only stopping to text his best friend and explain my 'hysterical job'. What followed were numerous 'hilarious' WhatsApp messages from various family members and friends about how I should now be called 'The Vagina Whisperer'.

After the 20th message pinged into my inbox, I had a complete meltdown and threw a Non-Disclosure Agreement in Patrick's face, telling him I could be sued for even telling him. (That's not actually true as Juliet had never made me sign a Non-Disclosure, unlike so many of my other clients. Since deciding what her husband's 'gift' was going to be, she had announced what she was doing to anyone who would listen, including the bemused-looking spotty teenager who served us coffee a week ago at Starbucks.)

Let's just say, she had no shame!

Having stormed out of the house, I had jumped on the tube to Hampstead and tried to diagnose the reason for my bad mood. I mentally ticked off the things in my head that might have been the reason.

Patrick? It annoyed me that he didn't put his empty tea mug in the dishwasher this morning but apart from that, he's fine (if a bit of an idiot for teasing me about my job).

Work? All of my clients at the moment were some of the loveliest mummies I could hope to work with and besides some rather bizarre requests (today's being top of the list), no one was really stressing me out that much.

Pregnancy? I stumbled over this one, mainly because I even felt bad for adding it to my list when we had tried so hard to get there in the first place. However, the more I let the word swill around in my brain, the more I knew it was the culprit of my foul temper.

When you are pregnant, people constantly say to you, 'Oh, how wonderful! You must be so excited?' or (my personal hate), 'You're absolutely glowing!' There is something about pregnant women that makes people think we are all ethereal and angelic, whereas, the truth be told, I have piles the size of gooseberries and my boobs are starting to leak milk. I tug at the material of my T-shirt cruelly stretched out over my belly and shift uncomfortably from one foot to the other.

God, I hate being pregnant.

Ping! A little cog turned in my head as this thought flitted through and I realised there and then the reason for my grumpiness: I was fed up of being pregnant. I was fed up of being fat and dumpy and needing to wee five times during the night. I was done with having to buy ANOTHER pair of maternity jeans because the last ones felt too tight or having to ask for my steak to be cooked 'well done' instead of lovely and juicy and raw. And last night, to make matters worse, Patrick and I had spent the evening at a friend's 'red wine and cheese' get together, neither of which I could eat or drink, thanks to me being pregnant, which resulted in me spending a torturous three hours nibbling on plain McVitie's crackers and sipping apple juice.

'Tiffany, can you pass Juno the instructions? They're over there on the side table.'

I'm snapped out of my discontent by Juliet's voice and a click of her fingers as she directs my eyeline to the vagina cast instructions on the table next to me.

'You MUST join in!' screams Juno, the hilarity of what is about to take place (plus the couple of glasses of champagne she has consumed whilst Juliet and I drink the non -alcoholic variety) has obviously just hit her.

'I might need a few more of these first!' I laugh, holding up my non-alcoholic champagne and cheers-ing the two friends. 'Plus, I'm not sure you could even find my bits under this bump!'

Whilst I am eight months pregnant, Juliet is only six and her bump is so neat and small, it doesn't seem to be hindering the vagina casting. Making my way into the kitchen on the pretence of topping up all of our glasses, I think back to the day when Juliet first mentioned the 'special gift for her husband'.

We had just been for a walk around a park, where I had followed her around on her power walk (complete with her dog, Snoopy), frantically writing notes as she monologued at me about the things she wanted done before the baby arrived: vagina casting was number 19 on the list.

'I saw it done on one of those awful reality TV show and thought it was hysterical so figured, why not do it? Frank will think it's hilarious and when I'm old and grey and have pushed three babies out of my vagina, I can look back and say, "Ah, that's what it used to look like. Those were the good old days!".'

I must admit, at the time I thought she was joking, but when an email arrived three days later, asking me if I'd found a casting kit yet, I realised the vagina cast was suddenly a top priority on Juliet's list. Having spent two full days calling around various artist studios in London (the majority of which went very quiet when I told them my request and one of them even hung up on me), I managed to locate a company in Brighton who were completely unfazed.

'Vaginas, penises . . . we've done them all. When do you want to book in?'

I'd be lying if I said I didn't very swiftly confirm that it wasn't me doing the cast. Within five minutes, Juliet's appointment had been made – her vagina was going to be well and truly 'plastered'.

Juliet then decided she wanted a test run. Which is why I am in her kitchen, taking a deep breath, ready to embark on the most bizarre day's work I have ever had. I walk back into the room. Juno is rolling around on the floor of the kitchen in hysterics, whilst Juliet is sitting, rather uncomfortably, on one of the kitchen chairs, legs akimbo. There are various paintbrushes and rubber gloves (not as dodgy as it sounds, I promise) scattered all over the floor and Juliet is clutching her sides in hysterics.

'Oh my God, Juno! I can't believe we're doing this. This is bloody fantastic! Why don't we do your boobs whilst we're at it? I'm sure there'll be enough plaster left!'

Juno throws a pillow in Juliet's direction and reaches for the champagne bottle.

'No chance! You're the pregnant one – we can blame your desire to do this on your mental hormones, but leave me out of it.'

I look at the screen in front of me and begin to smile. Juliet has mascara streaks running down her cheeks due to laughing so much. There is not a single part of her, right now, that is letting being pregnant stop her from having fun.

I should take some tips, I think to myself quietly. *Now's the time to stop moping about how tiresome being pregnant can be and instead embrace it.*

'OK, I'm in!' I bound over towards the others and grab a paintbrush and the set of instructions. 'But we're only doing my belly, nothing else.' I wave the paintbrush like an angry schoolmistress at Juliet and Juno. 'You can do what you like with your vaginas, but I'm keeping mine strictly under wraps!'

I have never laughed so much as I did the rest of that afternoon. Whilst I made myself scarce for the actual plastering bit (there's only so much I want to see of my clients' genitalia!), I could hear the screams of laugher and constant commentary from Juliet through the wall of the kitchen:

'So, the plaster's going on now – oh my fuck, it's cold! Juno, make sure you use the paintbrush – ouch, not like that! OK, have you used the plaster bandage? The instructions say you need to smooth the plaster with the paintbrush . . . Well, I can't bloody feel anything, I've a ton of concrete on my nether regions!'

An hour later and we're all staring in awe at the now-complete cast of Juliet's vagina.

'It looks . . .' Juliet's eyebrows are raised, a frown line appears between her eyebrows.

'Vagina-like?' I offer, before collapsing into fits of laughter.

We look at the mould in front of us – it's certainly no work of art – and conclude perhaps letting a professional do it is the best option. A wicked smile flickers across Juliet's face.

'Right, your turn.' She comes at me with a paintbrush and I run, screaming, out of the room. 'Show us your boobs so we can mummify them!' she shouts after me.

PART FOUR

THIRD TRIMESTER

Chapter 10

'There's only one rule: we don't want anything colourful, plastic or noisy. But apart from that, you have completely free rein.'

I looked over my notebook at the faces staring back at me to check they were joking. But it was blatantly obviously they were not.

Right, this one's going to be tricky, I thought.

My clients were Ashley and Miranda, who had just flown over from LA to deliver their baby at The Portland Hospital in central London. A week earlier, I had received an email from them, asking me to meet them at their South-bank penthouse so that we could 'discuss what they needed for the baby – and deck out the nursery'. I had felt a flush of fondness for this couple when I received their email – this was the sort of couple I loved working with. The ones who were genuinely excited about the arrival of their baby and wanted to be as prepared as possible ahead of the birth.

How wrong could I have been?

Five minutes earlier, I was greeted by an extremely pregnant Miranda as the doors of the lift opened directly into their penthouse. Expecting to have been met by a newly pregnant mummy (after all, most people start prepping for their baby the second the line on the pregnancy test appears), I was shocked to discover that she was actually nine months pregnant and one week past her due date.

Taking my hand, she proudly gave me a mini tour of their second home. The couple, despite living in LA, actually both came from New York and this was their first baby, Miranda informed me, as we moved into the living room, which had floor-to-ceiling windows enabling the lights of London to twinkle and dance on the glass. In the living space, an original curved Vladimir Kagan velvet sofa was combined with a woven ottoman pouf of Scottish wool, and in the far corner was a patinated brass wine and whisky unit. The huge dining table dominated in the middle of the room, setting the tone for what I could only presume were multiple social events – it was exquisite.

I was ushered out onto their private garden terrace and gasped out loud. There was an inside-outside water feature (a bit like a mini swimming pool) that connected the interior to a private garden terrace. On the terrace was a huge yet elegant fire pit, which was burning away in the summer evening haze. If I stood on tiptoes and looked to the left, I could even see the London Eye in the distance, its blue lights twinkling in the setting sun.

I don't think I had ever seen anything more beautiful.

But now wasn't the time to gawp. Taking my spot on the rattan garden sofa, draped with cashmere throws, I took out my notebook and waited expectantly to be given my instructions. Ashley handed me a blue folder with the words 'Baby Anderson' on it. My spirits soared slightly – maybe this was their 'to-do list' or their 'plan for the baby', but when I opened it, the file was completely empty.

'We had good intentions.' Miranda chuckled, whilst blowing on her recently painted nails. 'But things got so busy with work and life that we just didn't have time to commit to baby planning.'

I nodded – a lot of my clients have high-powered careers so I could understand the stress – but I must admit, deep inside, I had a sense of foreboding. She was, after all, due to 'pop' any minute and it seemed not even a single baby blanket or maternity bra had been purchased.

'So, we need you to get on top of everything. Plan it all out, deck out the nursery, order the baby stuff, book a baby nurse, you know. DO. EVERYTHING.' Ashley's New York drawl slid off his tongue confidently as he spoke – I could tell he was a man who was used to getting his own way. 'Money isn't an object. But we don't want anything colourful, plastic or noisy.'

'We've spent millions of dollars on this place,' Miranda butts in, making a sweep with her left arm, the diamonds on her wrist glittering in the evening sun. 'So, it cannot look as if a baby lives here. We don't want to lose ourselves and our style just because we are suddenly parents.'

I bit my lip and nodded. OK, so here we had a stereo-typical 'in denial' couple. Despite the bulging nine-month bump under Miranda's designer dress, there was absolutely no evidence anywhere that this couple were about to become parents. The teak bookshelf that I spotted on my walk through the living room contained only architectural books and luxury holiday guides, and instead of the coffee table being littered with 'baby magazines' and 'trimester to-do lists', it was completely bare, bar an expensive-looking letter opener from OKA.

It would have been so easy to judge this couple and label them 'devoid of all maternal and paternal instinct' but I couldn't help but feel that, although this was likely to be a challenge, I really wanted to help them. Through my years as a Mummy Concierge, I've learnt that sometimes couples really do bury their heads in the sand. Despite accepting that a baby will arrive at some point, they are determined to continue living the life they knew pre-pregnancy and become so determined in their wish to maintain this, they forget that having a baby means compromise and a lot of planning.

I was determined not to be fazed by the long 'to-do' list being shouted at me by Ashley, who was now in the sitting room. He was on a long-distance call to some film producer in LA, so his demands were interspersed with words such as 'unit base, recce and pre-call'. As he spoke, I made notes on my iPhone whilst simultaneously arranging them in priority order. Here's what it looked like:

1. Create list of swanky nursery furnishing brands – pass by A and M – and order in requested items.

2. Source wallpaper for nursery (no fluffy bunnies or elephants).
3. Find Moses basket and cot (neither to be traditional in style).
4. Babyproof the nursery.
5. Source vegan paint.
6. Arrange painter and decorator and electrician (only want them in the house between hours of 11 and 3pm).
7. Baby monitor and technical equipment must be out of sight.
8. Everything to be completed in two days.

Being faced with a couple who didn't want a nursery to detract from their impeccably designed home, I found myself in new and unforeseen territory. Whereas usually soon-to-be parents delight in ambling around baby shops, picking up minuscule baby grows and fawning over tiny teddy bears or bunny rabbits, I now had a family who wanted the complete opposite. There was no doubt they wanted their baby (I saw the way Miranda's eyes sparkled when I showed her some gorgeous booties I had just picked up for another client) and how Ashley unconsciously stroked her bump when he went to sit next to her, but they didn't want baby paraphernalia – which was going to make my job pretty tricky.

Two days later, I was back in their apartment and had banished Miranda and Ashley from returning until I called them to let them know I was finished. Silently praying Miranda's waters didn't break whilst they were out, I started work on the impossible – creating a nursery that would fit in with the stylish aesthetics of a home that looked as if it had never been frequented by a small child.

Earlier that morning, a huge delivery had arrived at the apartment. Around 20 boxes littered the empty space where the nursery would be, filled to the brim with everything from bouncers, monitors, cot bedding and lampshades to a Moses basket and stand, changing table and a baby play gym. The painter and electrician had just left, sweating and groaning under my sergeant major demands (but placated after several cups of tea sweetened with a mountain of sugar).

Where once there was slate grey wall (not at all baby friendly!), Joe the painter had done a fabulous job of covering every inch of industrial styling with a silk thread wallpaper that depicted small (and subtle) hot-air balloons in pastel pinks and blues. I had run my hand over it whilst walking towards the cot that had just been assembled and breathed out deeply. Everything about the wallpaper was luxurious – the thin shreds of silk were soft to touch and subtle blush pinks and cornflower blues melted into the background to create a complete sense of calm and relaxation.

The cot sat proudly in the bottom right-hand corner of the room, the sleigh bed design creating beautiful curves and a sense of softness that any baby would be happy to sleep in. The sheets were crisp and clean (and scented with lavender, which I had put through the iron last night after washing them so I knew they were void of any chemical nasties). At the bottom of the cot lay a hand-knitted blanket, embroidered with the baby's name, which Miranda and Ashley had let slip a couple of days before.

I had opted out of getting an actual baby changing table and had instead found a beautiful French antique dresser, which now had a changing mat on top and a simple white box stocked full of nappies, wipes and baby cream. Elegant in its simplicity, it sat just in front of the huge floor-to-ceiling window, which I had draped with muslin fabric to bring a sense of calmness to the room.

'I think we're all done here.' Martin, my expert baby-proofer, heaved himself up on his knees from his place on the floor and showed me his handiwork. Above him, opposite the cot, he had assembled a simple oak shelf with a baby monitor on top. He had just finished gathering up the wires and stapling them to the wall before covering them in cable tidy so that you could barely see them. He had also mounted all of the heavy furniture to the walls so that we didn't have to worry about an exploring baby and tumbling furniture. Everything looked immaculate. I smiled, pleased with our efforts and relieved that we might just about have pulled it off.

'What are you going to do about that?' Martin points towards the corner of the room and chuckles to himself. The offending item is my one rebellion. There, in all its glory, sits a baby gym, so loud and colourful, it's literally screaming for attention from us. From it dangles blue, red and green toys and at the bottom of the bouncer is a button that plays 60 minutes of nursery rhymes.

I was pretty certain that when the baby was born, that baby gym was going to be the thing they adored. So, I snuck it into the room in the hope that the parents were so overwhelmed by everything else that they would not notice it. Crossing my fingers, I smiled wickedly at Martin.

It's time for Ashley and Miranda to meet their baby's bedroom.

Hacks for setting up your nursery

1. **Make sure everything you could possibly need is within easy reach of the changing table.** Things such as nappies, wipes, baby cream, muslins and dummies need to be close by. The last thing you want is to step away from the baby and risk them rolling off because you need to grab something clean to slide under their bottom, post-poo explosion.

2. **Avoid clutter.** You'll be carrying a baby back and forth in the middle of the night and a misplaced chair (or playmat, toy, book, etc.) can be brutal to trip over when you're least expecting it.

3. **You can make any light a nightlight.** Just buy nightlight bulbs online and you can transform your favourite lamp into décor for your baby's room.

4. **Art makes a difference.** Framed prints that aren't themed or particularly babyish are a way of aligning all tastes and will last for many years of changes to come. So, consider artwork that will last a lifetime.

5. **Do decorate the ceiling.** Babies spend a lot of their time on their backs. Why not give your little one something to contemplate? Consider painting the ceiling a soothing colour or enhance your nursery theme with a mural or decals.

6. **Don't wait to babyproof the nursery.** Your baby may not be on the move yet, but before you know it, you'll have your very own toddling disaster zone. Take care to cover electrical outlets and tuck away cords. Anchor down any furniture that could pose a threat and secure rugs to the floor to prevent slips. Avoid hanging anything heavy on walls over where your baby is sleeping and keep hazardous objects and liquids out of reach of your baby's grabbing hands.

7. **Opt out of a dedicated changing table.** Babies grow quickly. One second they're in nappies, the next you'll find you're potty training. Consider buying a dressing table instead and popping a changing mat on top. That way, when you are done with nappies, you can use it for your baby's clothes.

8. **Think about storage options.** Consider buying a cot that has storage underneath, or, if it doesn't, invest in a storage drawer that can slide beneath the cot. You'll be amazed at how useful it will be for storing extra sheets and blankets.

9. **Make sure you have a parent area in the nursery,** complete with a comfortable nursing chair and a side table stacked with everything you will need during feeds so that they're in easy reach. This could include: a phone charger, a book/magazine, a lamp with a low lighting bulb in, tissues, a muslin.

10. **Don't scrimp on a mattress.** There's nothing wrong with accepting hand-me-down changing tables, wardrobes and baby clothes from friends or relatives. But when it comes to mattresses, always buy a new one because it's more hygienic. You'll never know how well a second-hand mattress was looked after or where it was stored. If you can, better to go new.

A few days later I received a bottle of champagne with a note attached. It simply said, 'You made every dream come true without us even realising it. Our baby has the most beautiful nursery in the world. Thank you.' I kept that note in my handbag for a week, and re-read it every time I wanted to smile.

Chapter 11

I never thought an average working Monday would begin with me waving a vibrator in the air and shouting out, 'Are you sure you want to take this to the hospital?' But that was exactly what happened when I was at a new client's house in Notting Hill, helping her pack her hospital bag.

A bump appeared around the doorframe, slowly followed by the rest of Ivy, her arms filled with what looked like hundreds of dresses.

'Oh, that was in my "maybe" pile . . . Let's go through that later. First of all, I want you to tell me which dress I should wear at the "Reveal".'

The 'Reveal', as Ivy had explained to me earlier that morning, was the moment when she and her husband would appear on the steps of the famous Lindo Wing, brandishing their brand-new baby for all to see. Since Kate Middleton and Prince William did this on the birth of their son George, it is now a request I get regularly from my clients and it no longer fazes me. If royalty can have a photo shoot opportunity on the steps of the hospital where their baby was born, then why can't mere mortals too?

Ivy dumped the pile of dresses onto her ornate four-poster bed before pulling out a tight black number that had what looked like shoelaces holding it together at the side. 'This is my Liz Hurley dress.' She ran a hand down it fondly. 'I got it the same year she wore it to the *Four Weddings* premiere – I was only 17 at the time and believe it or not, it still fits.'

I raised an eyebrow and glanced between Ivy's baby bump – she was eight months pregnant – and the dress – which looked like it was made using a piece of dental floss.

'Well, obviously it doesn't fit me NOW, but as soon as the baby is out, it will.'

I've heard this one before a lot and, taking a deep breath, I placed the vibrator I'd been holding back on the bed and patted the spot next to me, beckoning for Ivy to sit down.

'Ivy, you do know you're not going to snap back into shape immediately, right?' I kept my voice deliberately low and steady as I was slightly scared she might erupt when I explained the truth behind giving birth.

She looked at me blankly, so I took that as a sign to continue. 'You still look at least six months pregnant for a couple of weeks after you have a baby.' I watched as her eyebrows shot up to her forehead. 'And you'll have big sanitary towels in your knickers, so you probably won't want to be wearing anything skintight. Especially if you end up having stitches. We need to think about maternity bras, too.'

'Oh, I've sorted those.' Delving into a drawer next to her bed, she pulled out a lacy, hot-pink bra and G-sting. 'My mum always said you've got to wear nice underwear.'

I swallowed and stood up, running my hands down my jeans in a bid to remove any creases and look like I was in control.

'Ivy, let's start from the beginning again, shall we? Your hospital bag . . . here's the list.' I handed her a neatly printed-out list that I typed out specially for her the night before. Every time I work with a mummy on their hospital bag or baby kit, I always tailor it to the parents and their needs. It's so easy to just head to the internet and get a generic list, but I know from experience these lists never work. Every mother is different, every budget is different, and every birth is different – so there's no 'one- size-fits-all' hospital bag list. Which is probably why it is one of the most popular services that I offer.

I'm often asked what mums who come to me need help with most and it's always a difficult question to answer. Every mother has different concerns throughout her pregnancy – sometimes it can be the organisational aspect and wanting to feel in control of everything before the baby arrives, and for others, it's about understanding as much as possible what to expect once the baby is born and what options are around to help them. The majority of my clients initially come to me asking for a personalised 'maternity map', which involves me putting together a month-by-month guide on what they should be doing when, what appointments they should have booked, when their nursery should be finished by, when to start thinking about maternity nurses and so on. I think pregnant mothers can feel incredibly overwhelmed, so 90 per cent of my clients want someone who can say, 'Breathe – I'm here – this is what needs to be done and by when.' Others, such as Ivy, are often 'unique' in their demands.

I picked up the pink vibrator from her bed and waved it around my head.

'You need to explain this. Why on earth would you want a vibrator in the hospital when you are giving birth?' I threw it at her playfully and she exploded with laughter.

'I heard about these orgasmic births some women have and I thought if I bought my little friend along, it might help.'

I nodded my head in exasperation, smiling the whole time.

'OK, so that's one thing that you definitely DON'T need in your hospital bag.' I changed tack and adopted a soothing tone: 'Are you sure you're ready for how your life is going to be once the baby arrives? Did you go to that antenatal class I recommended?'

A few months ago, when Ivy first contacted me, she admitted she was the most clueless pregnant woman out there, so I had made it my mission to educate her as much as possible so she could feel confident and happy about becoming a mother. Since the beginning of her third trimester, I had been sending her daily 'maternity maps' in the hope she would be inspired. My maternity maps are essentially 'to-do' lists for each week of your pregnancy.

They might have important things on them, like booking in certain appointments with midwives, or getting a harmony test (a blood test that analyses the DNA of the fetus and has a detection rate of up to 99% for Down Syndrome), then sometimes I add in little jobs that I know that a particular client might like, such as going shopping for the first baby grow or booking in a pregnancy massage.

Ivy's maternity map had various things I knew she would love (I actually think she booked in three pregnancy massages at three different places around London!), but the one thing I had circled in red biro and drawn through with a yellow highlighter was 'attend an antenatal class'. I supplied her with a list of possible classes, outlining what sort of class they were: Posh Chelsea Mums Class, hypnobirthing-focused and so on.

I dug out Ivy's maternity map from my handbag and jabbed a finger at the spot on the paper. 'Did you go to any of these?'

Ivy looked up at me sheepishly and shook her head – 'I didn't really fancy it.' I felt the dread swell in my stomach. 'All that talk about blood and ripped vaginas and pooing during birth . . .' She shuddered dramatically from her place on the bed. 'It's not really "my thing".' She made quotation marks with her fingers as she said this and then closed her eyes dramatically.

OK, this woman needs educating – and fast.

* * *

Half an hour later, we have relocated to the home office, which is at the top of the house and has incredible floor-to-ceiling views over Holland Park. Ivy is ashen, her hands curled into tight balls in her lap and her mouth wide open in dismay. She is staring at my computer screen, where Rebecca, a wonderful antenatal teacher who I met years ago, is currently demonstrating how a baby's head fits through the pelvis. The problem is, Ivy has her eyes closed and is rocking manically backwards and forwards in her chair.

'OK, I honestly can't do this.' Her words come short and breathy and for a moment I think she might faint. I reach over and steady the chair for her, handing her a glass of water as I do so.

'Ivy, you need to face up to this. This is happening in a few weeks' time. You can't hide away behind designer dresses and six-inch stilettos. This baby is going to make an appearance and we need to make sure you're ready.'

I smile into the camera lens back at Rebecca and she grimaces nervously. I think we both know Ivy needs a LOT of training, and she needs it quickly.

'I'm just so worried.' Ivy raises a glass of water to her mouth and takes a big gulp. 'I know you probably think I'm ridiculous, but I'm worrying about stuff most mums probably don't worry about.' She looks at me nervously from the corner of her eye and kneads her shoulders with her hands.

I know what's about to happen as I see it with a lot of my clients: this is what I like to call 'The Mummy Moment'.

The Mummy Moment is those three minutes before a pregnant or new mummy is about to announce something that she is convinced is the most ridiculous thing you will ever hear. In those three minutes, she is likely to become flushed, agitated and embarrassed before blurting out whatever 'truth' it is she wants to convey to you. In Ivy's case, it's this: 'I'm mostly worried about tearing during birth and my vagina never being the same. What if Nick never wants to have sex with me again, or if my vagina hangs really low when I wear a swimming costume? What if I need so many stitches that my vagina will never be the same again? Nick might leave me, no man will ever want me again . . . I'll be a single mother with a saggy vagina.'

There are three ways to react to this. Option 1: Most people (I presume those who are not parents) might laugh and shake their heads whilst silently muttering, 'Thank God I'm not the one about to give birth!' I'm sure some of you are reading this right now and squeezing your thigh muscles tightly together, swearing internally that you'll never have a baby so you don't have to have a dialogue like this ever in your life.

Option 2 goes like this: There are those of you likely to be screaming at this page, saying, 'Get a grip! How vain can you be? Surely you should be worrying about the health of your baby, or how you're going to manage as a mother, rather than obsessing about your nether regions?'

And then there is Option 3: The Mummy Concierge option. You see, I've heard it all before and even if I haven't,

I'm never judgemental. Now, that's not me trying to be all 'holier than thou', it's just something that, over the years, I have realised is one of the must-have qualities if you're going to do a job like mine.

So, Ivy's greatest fear is her vagina and who am I to judge her for that? I have had some pregnant clients who are, faces as red as beetroot when they admit it, petrified of pooing during labour. There are others who admit to having piles (due to pregnancy constipation) so they have to hover over the sofa rather than sit on it because of the pain. I have even had a client who was so embarrassed by her linea nigra (the dark line some women get from their belly button to their pelvis when pregnant) that she booked weekly fake tanning sessions to disguise it.

You name it, I've heard it. It's easy to presume that the 'sensible' things to be worried about when you're pregnant are things like the pain of labour, or if you're going to be a good mother or not, but delve into a person's mind and you'll find that it's sometimes the 'little things' that cause the most stress. I had a client who had been scouring the internet to find a tummy button plaster – something she read about in an American magazine that states it will help 'push a protruding tummy button back into place'. (For those of you who don't know this, for some women during pregnancy, your uterus can push your tummy button forward regardless of whether you have an innie or an outie.) My particular client was paranoid that people could now see her 'outie' through her clothes and was desperate to find any solution to 'get it back to normal again'. After a bit of hand holding and tissues to wipe away tears, I confirmed to her that birth would in fact solve the problem as without a baby in there pushing on her uterus, her tummy button would happily revert back to an innie.

The 'Never the Same Again Vagina' debacle was one I dealt with a lot too.

'Ivy, let's book you an appointment with your midwife so she can talk you through everything and answer all of your questions about your vagina.' Ivy winced as I said the word. 'Millions of women give birth every day and their vaginas all remain intact – if not a little bruised for a few weeks. And I'm pretty sure Nick will be so in awe of you for birthing his baby, he'll be holding you in a hero status light and won't give a crap about what's happening below.'

Again, another sentence I never thought would be a part of my daily vocabulary, but there we go.

The one thing I have learnt about pregnant women is that no worry should ever be dismissed. I live by the motto 'You Do You' and this transcends throughout pregnancy, birth and beyond. Just because one mother might be worried about something truly serious during her pregnancy (she could have a health issue, for example, or may be having a difficult pregnancy), it doesn't mean that other mothers' worries, (torn vaginas, pregnancy farting or haemorrhoids) are any less valid. As people, we are all different – we all wear different clothes, live in different homes, choose to spend our Saturday nights differently – but when it comes to pregnancy, people suddenly feel pressured to fit into one pregnancy category. I completely disagree with this – all mothers are different, all pregnancies are different, all babies are different. There is no one hard-and-fast rule that fits and works for everyone. If I could have 'you do you' tattooed on my forehead for whenever I visited a new mother, I would. It's a phrase that I genuinely believe could help every pregnancy, birth and life beyond.

* * *

It's getting dark when Ivy and I finally finish putting the last items in her hospital bag. Her call with Rebecca finished an hour earlier and having laid all her fears on the table, Rebecca and I had set about dispelling them all and making sure she felt more comfortable about what lay ahead. Her hospital bag, no longer brimming with inappropriate outfits or buzzing vibrators, was now packed neatly and sensibly with garments for her baby carefully folded into Ziploc plastic bags (a tip I learnt many years ago, which saves tired and emotional parents from scurrying around in the bag, trying to find that rogue baby mitten or hat).

Ivy also has a fully packed toiletries bag complete with not only the necessities such as toothbrush and deodorant, but those little things that I have learnt along the way can really help you post-birth: mint tea bags in case she ends up having a C-section (mint tea is great for relieving trapped wind pain that accompanies abdominal surgery), earplugs to dull out the noise of a busy hospital ward and aroma-therapy pillow spray to disguise the chemical hospital smell that Ivy admitted sent her into spasms of panic.

'And you're going to need this.' I hand Ivy the small grey donkey toy, which she had proudly shown me a few weeks ago, insisting it was going to be the baby's new best friend and first ever teddy.

I always tell my mummies to take the first toy with them into the hospital. That way, you can take that first photo of your baby with the toy next to them and then years later, when they are pulling the toy around by its ears and it's covered in dirt and its hair has rubbed off due to so many cuddles, you can show your child how small they once were, lying next to it.

Ivy draws a hand across under her eye and pulls me into a hug. 'I couldn't have done this without you.'

Embarrassing things every pregnant person worries about (but rarely admits) and how to deal with them

1. **Stretch marks** – There's no denying when you are pregnant you are likely to get some of these silvery lines across your belly and/or hips. Nine out of ten women get them because the elastin in the skin stretches as you gain weight.
   Mummy Concierge hack: Invest in some stretch mark cream the second you get the positive on the pregnancy test and apply every morning and evening.

2. **Farting** – The hormone progesterone is your baby's best friend but can lead to embarrassing problems for you. Lots of women admit to farting a lot more during pregnancy and this can be something that causes a great deal of stress.
   Mummy Concierge hack: Wear loose clothing (hello, pregnancy jeans!) and keep a food diary to identify triggers.

3. **Itchy nipples** – Pregnancy usually equals a bigger set of boobs but because breasts become engorged, they can itch too.

Mummy Concierge hack: Breasts will grow throughout pregnancy so it's easy to end up with a badly fitting bra, which can lead to rubbing and itching, so make sure you get regular bra fittings to help.

4. **Leaky bladder** – Another one of those pregnancy nightmares is that a simple sneeze or cough can lead to an unexpected leak.

   Mummy Concierge hack: Practise working your pelvic floor every time you brush your teeth or when there's an advert break on TV. How? Pull up on the correct muscles (the ones you switch on to avoid passing wind in public!).

5. **Haemorrhoids** – Swollen, itchy or bleeding veins around the rectum occur because the veins are more relaxed.

   Mummy Concierge hack: They should go away once baby arrives but in the interim, eat high-fibre foods, drink lots of water and avoid standing for long periods.

6. **Pooing during birth** – Look, there's no denying it might happen (pushing a baby out is the same sensation as having a poo!).

   Mummy Concierge hack: If it does happen, the likelihood is that only the midwife will notice. The good thing about this? A midwife will have seen and dealt with this a million times (if not more) and she will subtly dispose of it without any drama. Most women don't even realise it has happened.

7. **Partner being put off after giving birth** – Lots of women are really worried about their partner going 'off' them after witnessing birth. After all, how can they look at a vagina the same way again if a baby has squeezed out of it?

   Mummy Concierge hack: If you're worried about your partner's reaction to being at the birth, the two of you need to discuss it. If you're still concerned, ask them to stay at the 'top end'. They can offer just as much support wherever they decide to stand or sit and you need to feel comfortable with this.

Chapter 12

An email pinged into my inbox from a client that immediately had me intrigued. A friend of mine, Anna, had sent the following:

> Woo hoo! I've been accepted! The powers-that-be have deigned me both elite and stylish enough to attend the best-kept mummy secret in west London. Details below!

Below the email was a beautifully crafted invite welcoming Anna to 'The Bumps Tribe'. (Yes, I've changed the name so as to keep their top-secret, only-in-the-know 'members' club' as exclusive as it still is.) I raised my eyebrows and smiled inwardly as I read the email – this is just so typical of Anna. When she moved to Chelsea ten years ago, she vowed to experience everything west London had to offer and immediately signed up to every private members' club and celebrity infused gym, making sure to frequent *Tatler*'s must-eat Chelsea restaurants at least once a week. Let's just say she embraced the 'Sloaney' lifestyle and certainly wasn't going to let a pregnancy bump get in the way of that.

Scanning the rest of the email, I digest the fact that not only is this seemingly an incredible elite club (rumour has it mummies-to-be are secretly 'vetted' before their membership is granted), but it is also actually an antenatal class for the rich and famous who live in the Royal Borough of Kensington and Chelsea. Intrigued, I log on to their website and digest what 'The Bumps Tribe' actually is.

Run by two 'Yummy Mummies' (their photos on the website confirm this), this antenatal class seemed very different to your typical NCT class that most parents sign up to. Whereas NCT focuses on birth – and encourage natural births and breastfeeding – this luxury class takes place over eight weeks. Each week, mothers are taught by top industry professionals – from midwives and obstetricians to nutritionists, physiotherapists and GPs. The more I read, the more intrigued I become, and I swiftly send off an email asking if I can be included in their upcoming class.

The 'vetting' process must have been one of those nasty rumours because just a week later, I received a reply, inviting me to attend the next bump course, which is to start in a few weeks' time. I can't wait. Not only is it a great opportunity for me to learn about what life with a baby has in store for me, but also a wonderful chance to see if this is a service I can recommend to my pregnant clients.

* * *

As I step out of the Underground at South Kensington station, I glance down at the map on my phone and stride purposefully towards the stucco period house where the first class is being held. Everything about South Kensington is highly polished, from the well-heeled, often famous residents to the fact that most clothes shops have items starting at £600. Thankfully, as I have lived in neighbouring Chelsea for many years, I am used to the glamour and glitz, but nothing can quite prepare me for the prestige that was this antenatal class.

The door is opened by the epitome of a yummy mummy – who as it turns out is also our hostess. She is wearing skinny jeans teamed with Prada loafers and a white T-shirt, which I'm sure I spotted in the window of Whistles earlier. Around her shoulders is a leopard print scarf, adding a cool yet relaxed look to her stylish outfit. I immediately wish I had dressed up more and made a bit more effort with my make-up. Clearly a dash of mascara and a hint of blusher isn't going to cut it here.

I follow her into her home (yes, the class is actually held within her £2m house) and am offered a glass of sparkling homemade elderflower cordial before being shown where the downstairs loo is ('I know how much pregnant women need to pee!' she laughs). The downstairs loo is the size of my current living room. All over the walls are photos of the hostess's family. Being slightly nosy, I flick from one photo to the next, noticing that everyone has a different well-known celebrity or socialite in it.

When I emerge, smelling of Bamford hand wash, I am ushered into the living room, where the rest of my 'Bumps Tribe' await. Smiling at each one nervously, I sit myself down on a free sofa (there are four sofas in this room) and introduce myself to one of the mothers next to me. We are all heavily pregnant and before too long the conversation becomes more relaxed as we chat about pregnancy pains and if we know what sex the baby is. The mothers in this room are all definitely from a certain social set. Nearly everyone has a neat designer handbag by their feet and engagement rings the size of planets. As I quietly eavesdrop on nearby conversations, I hear talks about second homes in St Tropez, the best Botox doctor in London and the latest exclusive members' club that costs £5,000 just to join.

It would be so easy to sit here and judge, but I also notice something else about all of these women. Every single one of them is cradling their bump and has an air of nervousness about them. Even the woman opposite me, who is loudly bleating on about potential childcare when her baby is born, stops every now and again and takes a deep anxious breath, looking down at her stomach apprehensively.

That's when it hits me – no matter who these women are, where they're from or what kind of privileged upbringing they've had, we all have one solid thing in common: we are about to embark on a new life that we know NOTHING about. We are about to become mothers to a tiny child who will rely solely on us. And right here, right now, we just don't know what to expect. Which makes this the perfect moment for our host, Iona, to step into the room and introduce herself properly. A hush descends over the group as she begins to tell us what to expect from our class.

'We don't want to freak you all out, but in this class we will discuss all the elements of giving birth and tell you what to expect in the ensuing weeks,' she says, making sure she makes eye contact with each and every one of us. 'There is so much pressure on mothers to be perfect, we want to give you realistic expectations of your new role and the inevitability of nature's imperfections.'

My hands have become very clammy and I subtly try to wipe them on my jeans.

Goodness, this is all feeling very serious.

'You'll notice that we didn't offer for you to bring your partners along to these classes,' she continues, flicking a strand of her hair which has fallen across her face out of her eyes. 'That's because we are going to talk about everything – leaking nipples, vaginal tears, diet, fitness, sex. Nothing is out of bounds. And because of this, these classes are a partner-free zone. We want you to be able to open up and tell us the things that are really worrying you so we can put your mind at rest.'

She goes on to introduce the experts who will be talking to us today. A young-looking midwife, who introduces herself as Kelly, explains that she has delivered over 600 babies and is herself a mother-of-three. A local GP from a Chelsea practice nods her greeting at us and then explains she will talk about post- and pre-natal depression. We are then greeted by a women's physio, who promptly starts the class by asking us all to squeeze our pelvic floor muscles in unison (and much to our embarrassment). The reason for this? 'I bet at least ten of you in this class [side note, there are only ten women in total in the class] are worried, whether you admit it or not, about having a baby through your vagina and it feeling flabby and gaping the next time you have sex with your husband. Pelvic floor exercises will make sure this doesn't happen.'

We all laugh nervously, but I must admit, I make a note of the pelvic floor trainer she recommends in my notepad.

As the class progresses, I notice that conversation and advice is far removed from what I had expected an 'average' antenatal class to be. We talk about things like having your baby privately, night nurses, nannies, long-haul travel with newborns, etc. without anyone raising an eyebrow. It is without a doubt that this class is tailored to a certain type of person, a 'high-end' type of mother. Someone who wants to be able to breastfeed wearing Prada and is determined that life won't change too much after their baby (due to the fact they will probably have LOTS of hired help in one of their many homes).

We leave the class three hours later, exhausted, slightly freaked out (the midwife showed us photos of a torn vagina), but mentally more prepared for what is to come. A couple of the mothers suggest a 'skinny caffè latte in a café nearby' but I decline, instead agreeing to be added to the Bumps Tribe WhatsApp group and joining them all for brunch the following week.

It's only when I get home an hour later that I digest what I had just been through. And I admit, I was scared. Not due to the expensive highlights, the air that smelled of perfume or the surgically enhanced pouting lips that surrounded me these last couple of hours. I was scared of what was about to come. Of birth. Of being a mum. Of all of the things that had been mentioned to us in our class that 'might not turn out the way we expect'.

Chapter 13

When I received the message from Olivia, I was worried. Coming from a normally fly-by-the-seat-of-your-pants type woman, oozing confidence and laughing at everything with an intense freedom, the text seemed uncharacteristically subdued and sad:

> I don't know if it's normal to request this – but can you meet me? Currently sat in my car and can't stop crying.

Pulling up on the country road, with Olivia's car parked in front of me, I swiftly turned off the car ignition and grabbed my coat, jumping out of the front seat. Olivia spotted me in her rear-view mirror and leant over to open her passenger car door. It had started raining a few minutes before, so I held my coat up over my head and scrambled into the car. Once cocooned inside, with the heater blaring, I wiped the raindrops from my face to see a visibly upset Olivia. Her eyes were swollen and clots of mascara were running down her face. I had met Olivia numerous times before and usually she took great pride in her appearance – she was always expertly made up and wore beautiful clothes. Today, she was sitting in her car in a baggy sweater (I presumed it must be her husband's) and black worn-looking leggings.

'Oh, my goodness, what's wrong? Is it the baby?' I pulled her in to me for a hug, fearing what she was about to tell me.

Olivia and her husband Geoff had been trying for a baby for three years now. They really had been through it all. Having started trying the second they were married and hoping desperately for a 'honeymoon baby' which didn't come, having a baby had become a full-time obsession. Eight months after trying naturally, they had visited their doctor, who referred them to a fertility specialist. The next three years were spent going back and forth to fertility appointments, numerous attempts at IUI, Olivia having her fallopian tubes flushed, injections, tablets, hormones and eventually three rounds of IVF, the final one resulting in a successful pregnancy.

'It's not the baby, the baby's fine.' Gulping in air between sobs, she wiped the tears away from her eyes, smudging her mascara even more. 'It's me and Geoff. I'm not sure we're going to make it.'

I feel something thump in the pit of my stomach and take Olivia's hand.

Please don't tell me that all the stress of trying to get pregnant has now broken their relationship. I couldn't bear it.

'OK, let's start from the beginning.' I gather up my coat from the floor of the car and reach into the back to grab

Olivia's. 'But first, we need some air. Come on, let's talk and walk.'

* * *

Olivia lived in the Cotswolds, an area I had visited lots throughout my years, so I knew the public footpaths well. The rain had eased slightly and the sun was attempting to make an appearance behind some clouds, so I led her down one of the little country lanes that went into one of the big country estates in Oxfordshire. The walks around here were beautiful and even if I couldn't solve Olivia's problems there and then, a bit of fresh air was bound to do her some good.

Ten minutes later and Olivia has told me the reason she thinks it might be over for her and Geoff. 'I just don't want sex anymore.' She shudders as she says this, covering her eyes with her hands, embarrassed. 'I don't know what it is. When we first met, we had the best sex life ever – we'd be doing it anywhere and everywhere, and we both loved it. But now, I can't even bear it when he touches me. I clam up and push him away.' She looks up at me, tears filling her eyes again. 'The thing is, I love him so much. I just don't want to have sex – with him, or anyone. What's wrong with me?'

After a little bit more delving into the relationship, I conclude that early that morning, Geoff and Olivia had had a huge argument. Geoff had woken early and leant over in bed to give Olivia a 'cuddle', which she promptly pushed away. He then got emotional – asking her why she no longer wanted to have sex with him and if she still loved him. The argument had increased as emotions rose and culminated with Olivia running out of the house and driving away.

'I just needed to get away, to process my thoughts. What do you think is wrong with me, Tiffany? Do you think we need to divorce?'

* * *

I wish I could say Olivia was the first mum who has come to me with this question, but unfortunately, that's not the case. When I first set up my business, I knew there would be a huge element of hand holding and reassuring attached to being a Mummy Concierge. Pregnant women are full of hormones and I was used to receiving regular anxiety-ridden text messages or phone calls, but something I was seeing so much more often was the serious emotional impact that trying for a baby and fertility treatments were having on couples.

As Olivia continued to outline to me how she was feeling, an uneasy feeling settled deep down in my stomach and flashbacks from a few years ago played out in front of my eyes. I remembered the day Patrick and I were due to attend a friend's one-year-old's birthday party. That morning, I had peed on an ovulation test, which had announced

I was ovulating. I was furious. Why? Because a) we were due at the park in under three minutes so there was absolutely no way we could fit in a quick session in time and b) Patrick was leaving the party early to catch a flight to New York for the next five days for work.

Ultimately, it meant that our chance of conceiving that month was now impossible.

Patrick and I had argued – fiercely. I told him his work was more important than us having a baby and he told me, 'We can always try next month,' which made me even more angry and emotional. At the time, every month was a gift – a chance to conceive the baby we had for so long been hoping for – and to me, delaying it by a month felt like missing a potential golden opportunity.

I went to the children's party – alone – and 15 minutes into it, a friend found me sobbing behind a bush. 'It's just so hard being around all of these babies when I don't know if I will ever have one,' I yelled, loudly enough for other people in the park to turn around. 'No one knows what it's like trying to have a baby when everyone else around you pops them out so easily. I just can't bear it!'

'The thing is, I'm pregnant already, so I don't understand why my sex drive isn't just back to normal. We have what we have always wanted yet sex still feels so regimented and alien to me.' Olivia had sat down now and was idly plucking blades of grass between her fingers. She looked so sad and distraught, I desperately wanted to help.

'Olivia, have you ever actually thought about how much you went through trying to get pregnant?' I spoke softly, furrowing my brow as I tend to do when I'm saying something serious. 'You scheduled sex for four and a half years. Every time you ovulated it was like a beacon saying, "Whip your kit off and get down and dirty".' Olivia didn't look up, but she smiled as I said this. 'I mean, talk about pressure! No wonder sex is now something you don't enjoy. When you were trying for a baby, it was like being in the army – every kiss and fondle dictated by a bloody ovulation kit.' I plucked a piece of grass from the ground in front of me and tossed it away aggressively. 'I remember that feeling so well. It's AWFUL.'

'But that was then.' Olivia looked up at me solemnly. 'I'm pregnant now and I still don't want sex. Surely that must mean we – myself and Geoff – are broken?'

A solo tear slid down her face and I saw her body crumple.

'Olivia, look at me. Lots, and I mean LOTS, of women feel like this. When sex is a means to an end, you can forget it can be fun! I think you've probably associated sex with trying to get pregnant – and all of those horrific emotions attached to that – so no wonder you're struggling with getting back into it.'

'But what can I do? How can I change it?' The desperation in Olivia's voice was heart-wrenching and in that moment I decided to do something to help. Just because my repertoire usually involved prepping for a baby, it didn't mean I couldn't also try to help when there were relationship problems too.

'Right . . .' I whipped out a pen and notepad from my handbag and sat cross-legged on the ground, a determined look on my face. 'Tell me all the things you enjoy doing and all the things Geoff loves.'

Olivia laughed and looked at me questioningly, her right eyebrow raised slightly.

'No, I don't mean sex wise!' I burst into fits of laughter and Olivia joined in, perhaps thrilled that I wasn't about to quiz her on her favourite sexual positions. 'I mean, what do you love doing together? What did you used to do before you were trying to have a baby?'

As Olivia started talking, I scribbled down everything she was saying, a feeling of hope surging throughout my body.

I could do this; I was going to help.

* * *

A few weeks later, my phone buzzed whilst I was in the middle of a meeting with a new Baby PR company. Glancing down, I smiled and excused myself. I left the room and typed in Olivia's mobile number. She answered on the second ring.

'Oh, my goodness, Tiffany. I can't thank you enough! This is EXACTLY what we needed.'

At this, I smiled. I had spent the last couple of weeks arranging a babymoon for Olivia and Geoff, which Olivia liked to refer to secretly as 'our get-back-in-the-sack' trip. I'm certainly no relationship psychologist, but seeing the way Olivia was the day I met her in her car, I knew I had to help arrange something to get them out of their rut. Some of her friends apparently started referring to it as the 'sex trip', but I was determined that it was going to be so much more than that. Armed with Olivia's list of things that she and Geoff liked doing, I had set about arranging a weekend away for them to enjoy doing all the things they loved before trying to get pregnant, but also have time to reflect on the fact they were going to be parents very soon.

I heard the 'ding' of a photo being delivered to my phone and saw that Olivia was sending me some snaps from her trip. She and Geoff were booked into Limewood Hotel, an oasis of a place in the New Forest surrounded by wild ponies and a stone's throw away from some beautiful beaches. In every photo that arrived onto my phone, Olivia was grinning from ear to ear and I laughed out loud as she sent a snap of the list I had sent her and big red 'ticks' next to them.

1. Relive your first date – a picnic on the beach.
2. A pregnancy massage for you and hot stones for him (Olivia had confided in me that Geoff never gets massages because he thinks they are a bit 'feminine', so we booked him in for something different to see how he fared).
3. Attend a cookery lesson (Limewood has an amazing cookery course, which I had managed to get them on.

Geoff and Olivia actually met at a work gala, where they bonded over their love of Italian food – and the course just happened to be all about making homemade pasta!).

4. Attempt fly fishing – this was on Geoff's wish list, but judging by the photo that Olivia just sent, she seemed to have grabbed the bull by the horns. The smile on her face and the impressed grin on Geoff's showed that she had obviously done a very good job!

Looking over my shoulder to check that the PR lady was not getting frustrated at my absence, I quickly typed out another text: 'Have you popped the balloon yet?'

The balloon was the final surprise I had arranged for their little getaway/babymoon. Having um-ed and ah-ed about finding out the sex of their baby, the couple eventually decided to find out. Three days previously, I had popped into the hospital to meet with their obstetrician and collect the piece of paper that told us the sex. I then dashed across London to a balloon company and explained the situation, whereupon they filled a big black balloon with 'boy or girl?' written on it with appropriately coloured confetti. All that had to happen now was for Olivia and Geoff to 'pop' it and reveal the sex of their baby.

An hour later, I got the photo and the text I'd been waiting for: a euphoric Olivia standing under a popped balloon, pink confetti flying everywhere: 'Thank you. Mummy Concierge to the rescue again. PS. Where did you hide the condoms?'

Mistakes people make when trying to conceive

1. Most women know they should start taking pre-natal vitamins once they're pregnant but few know you should actually start taking folic acid six months before conception. This will give your body enough time to build up folic acid levels.

2. Most women assume when they are having trouble getting pregnant that it's solely their 'fault'. This is not true, so it's really important to not only have yourself checked over but also your partner, by a medical professional.

3. Another common mistake is waiting too long to talk to your doctor. If you're under the age of 35 and have been trying for a baby for more than a year, it's time to check in with your doctor. If you're over 35 and you've been trying for six months, it's time to seek help. It's worth knowing that women aged under 40 should be offered three cycles of IVF treatment on the NHS (provided you meet certain conditions) and women over 40 are offered just one round.

4. A common mistake is waiting till after you've ovulated to have sex. At this point you've probably missed your window – you actually want to have sex in the days

leading up to ovulation, about three to four days, and one to two days after. This is because sperm lives in the body for up to 72 hours and once an egg is released, it only has about 24 hours of viability, so it's really important to identify when you are ovulating.

5. Don't stress out! I know, a hard one. It can be very easy to get worked up and stressed if you don't get pregnant right away, but it's important to note that only 20 per cent of couples who will ultimately have a successful pregnancy get pregnant each month – you're not alone.

Chapter 14

The text message simply said, 'Very clever'. I squint at my phone and re-read the message again: Very. Clever.

Leaning back on my sofa, I picture Patrick halfway across the word, an amused smirk on his face as he digests what I have just sent him. As is always the case with me, when met with sarcasm or a disbelief in my ideas, I puff up my chest and attack:

'I can hear the sarcasm 5,000 miles away. Please turn the volume down. I personally think it's a brilliant name and is exactly what they are looking for.'

I wait, feeling more and more agitated until his reply pops up on my phone:

'Like I said, it's very clever.'

Feeling the frustration well up inside me, I stab in his phone number and try to control my breathing (in, out, in, out) until he picks up.

'Tiff, please don't start getting all uppity. It's clever.'

'But it's got to be MORE than clever!' I shout back. 'It needs to be unique and powerful, beautiful, but not pretentious . . . Jeez, Patrick, I'm stressing out here!'

* * *

Let me update you. Three weeks ago, I was contacted by a new client with one of the more 'unique' parenting requests I have to deal with every now and again. Sophia was incredibly direct when I asked her how I could help.

'I need a baby name,' she explained with no hint of what was about to come. In fact, she sounded incredibly relaxed, as though she had just called up a shop and asked if they stocked baked beans.

'OK, sure.'

I smiled down the phone and tried not to give anything away in my voice. Sometimes mothers do contact me with strange requests, but I had a feeling in the pit of my stomach that this was just the start.

'Would you like me to recommend some wonderful baby name books? Or perhaps you want to pass some potential names by me and we can have a think about the pros and cons?'

'No. I need a name. And YOU have to come up with it. And I have a list of must-haves. Have you got a pen?'

Panicked (it was only 7am, after all), I threw open my bedside drawer and rifled around, desperately hoping there might be a pen in there somewhere. There wasn't, so I made do with a blunt eyeliner pencil. Opening the book I was currently reading, I flicked to a clean page and scribbled: Baby Name. Must-haves.

Baby Names Must-Haves:
- Must be a name that sounds endearingly cute as a baby, but powerful and successful as a man

- Must sound beautiful and lyrical
- Must have a cute nickname/abbreviation
- Must be completely unique (ideally, never used before)
- Easy to spell
- Easy to pronounce
- Looks lovely when written down

Baby Names Must-Nots:
- Be a name used by any current friends or colleagues
- Be the name that any celebrity has used
- Start with A, G or J
- Sound pretentious
- Rhyme with anything 'smutty'
- Have too much alliteration in it
- Must not end with an S
- Must not sound too masculine or too feminine
- Be too short
- Be too long (seven letters max)
- Be American (wants Baby to have a name that sounds regal)

Two weeks later and I'm running late for my first meeting with Sophia. Usually, with my VIP clients, I set aside a whole day for them (even if they just booked a one-hour meeting) as I know that demands can go far beyond what they originally asked for. I had a client a few months earlier who booked me for a one-hour consultation at 9am and at 5pm we were still walking around Harrods, gathering up suitable baby toys for her unborn baby's nursery.

I spot her before she sees me. As it's a sunny day, she is sitting in the outside terrace of the café in central Chelsea. She is surrounded by a plethora of shopping bags and I can clearly spot the names of some of the most premium shops in west London: Liz Earle, Browns, Harvey Nichols. As I sit down, she wafts a box in front of me and simply says, 'For you.'

I accept it gracefully, trying to act as though this happens all the time. She nods at me in a way that gives permission for me to open it, so I do and I can't help but gasp out loud:

'Sophia, I can't accept this.'

'Well, you must. I've had it engraved so I can't take it back.'

I pull out a beautiful leather-bound Smythson's notebook and run my hand over it carefully. I resist the urge to bring it to my nose and smell it – I can't imagine Sophia would be too impressed. Turning it over in my hands, I see that on the front are the words 'Baby Notes' and on the bottom right-hand corner are my initials: 'TLN'

'Oh, Sophia, this is just beautiful! I can't believe you remembered I was pregnant. Oh, thank you!' The words spill from my mouth appreciatively. 'I've actually just been for a scan and—'

She cuts me off before I can finish.

'For your baby? Oh no, I'm sorry, but I've misled you. This book is for you to write all your notes on OUR baby. I figured as you are finding the best for our little one, then you need the best notebook in which to write everything in.'

OK. So, this is something I'm going to have to get used to. VIP clients are VIPs for a reason. And that reason is that everything has to be about them.

Noted.

Despite the confusion, I am still thrilled with my new notebook and eagerly fish out a biro from my handbag and write 'BABY NAMES' on the first page. Then I fill Sophia in on my plan.

Having chatted with her numerous times over the last couple of days, I had begun to realise that just 'suggesting' baby names was not going to cut it. The hours I had spent trawling through baby name books and researching names on Google had come to nothing. A swift 'no' and a shake of the head from Sophia on our Zoom calls had made me realise that I needed to pull out the big guns.

'We've got a couple of people coming to join us today,' I start, nervously playing with my handbag strap under the table. 'I've handpicked a group of leading experts so we can all get together and brainstorm some potential names.'

Sophia nods and leans forward, eager to hear more. Maybe I have actually nailed this idea.

'We have a whole bunch of creatives and people who I have worked with in the past.'

As I'm speaking, I feel a hand on my shoulder and spin around to see my group of 'baby name experts' gathering behind me. There is an explosion of colour suddenly on the terrace – a sea of burnt orange blazers, an extravagant peacock feather hat and horn-rimmed spectacles. You can see just from looking at them that these people are all creatives. A surge of hope zooms through my body: today we are going to find the perfect baby name.

As my experts take their seats around our narrow table, I swiftly introduce them to Sophia and explain their expertise. We have the creative director of a top advertising company, a mummy blogger, a linguistic expert and a poet. Looking Sophia directly in the eye, I continue. 'I figured that getting lots of creative brains in one room might mean we can narrow down a potential list to start considering.'

She nods enthusiastically and I can see that she is impressed – I have proved to her that I have gone above and beyond.

Two hours later and we have a list. Some of the names are certainly 'out there' and a huge majority have to be discarded due them not following the previously laid-out rules of 'must-haves' and 'must-nots'. I pass the list to Sophia.

'So, the next step is a focus group,' I explain carefully, tilting my head towards Sophia and trying to gauge her reaction. 'It's something that is traditionally used by marketing companies to see what people think of a certain product. We will put this list of names' – I point to the piece of paper in her hand – 'to a group of strangers and gauge their reaction.'

Sophia looks confused. 'But why do I want strangers choosing my baby's name?' she asks, rightly so.

I place a hand on hers in what I hope is a soothing gesture. 'It's just a way for you to see how people react to the names and it might help you rethink and consider situations and names you might not have liked initially.'

Sophia throws back her highlighted hair and laughs. 'Let's do it!' she says, a huge smile spreading across her beautifully chiselled face. 'But I'm definitely NOT calling my child Leaf,' she adds, playfully nudging Julian, our poet. 'Even if it does "suggest that he will sail through life like a leaf on a stream".' We all laugh, catching each other's eyes as we do so and smiling conspiratorially at Julian. Even I had to agree with that; Leaf was definitely one of the more left-field suggestions.

* * *

A month later, Sophia calls me to let me know her little boy has been born. So, did she take the name suggested by the focus group? Of course not!

'In the end, we decided to go with something traditional and so we called him Richard.' I put my hand to my forehead in exasperation – after all that hard work! 'Did you know it's the name of a king in one of Shakespeare's plays?' she continues, oblivious to the months of hard work that had just gone down the drain. 'And in the end, my parents couldn't get to grips with having a grandson with a name they couldn't pronounce so Baby Richard it is!'

I smile into the receiver and shake my head from side to side, a huge smile appearing on my face.

'Well, I suppose you always have a second name to think about,' I suggest, playfully.

'Oh, that's sorted already. We actually quite liked "Leaf" as a suggestion so he's Richard Leaf Harrison . . .'

PART FIVE

BIRTH

Chapter 15

I had already been in Selfridges for over three hours, my arms full of designer dresses, silk pyjamas, various lotions and potions and a designer handbag which was going to double as a nappy bag. Harriet was a new client of mine who was also mum to two-year-old Edward (who was currently wrapping his sticky hands around my legs whilst we waited for his mummy to try on yet another outfit).

'How is that one looking?' I ask cautiously.

Let's just say, Harriet seemed highly strung today. When I met her outside Oxford Street tube a couple of hours ago, she had Edward in a rugby hold in her left arm and was barking instructions into her mobile phone at the pace of an Olympic sprinter. When she saw me, she physically breathed a sigh of relief, bundled Edward into my arms and marched off towards Bond Street, beckoning for me to follow with a flick of her finger.

'Mummy cross,' said Edward, looking up at me with his big blue eyes before pointing at the retreating back of his mother. 'Me draw on her dress and she cry.' He knitted his brows together and pulled an exaggerated frown.

He's so sweet, I think, as we weave our way through the tourists to catch up with Harriet. *I can't believe I'm going to have my own little boy in just a few weeks. Bliss!* Little did I know that at that exact moment he was also smearing thick red jam from his sandwich down the back of my cream cashmere dress. Had I realised, it would have set the tone perfectly for the rest of the day.

'It's just goddamn AWFUL!' Harriet appeared from behind the thick plum-coloured curtain and stood in front of me, pawing at the material around her pregnant belly and grimacing. 'I mean, just look at it. I look HUGE! And these' – she cups her breasts and bounces them up and down – 'look like something that should belong on a cattle farm. Right, let's try the Versace.'

I looked down at my own 8-and-a-half-month-pregnant bump and sighed. I completely understood how Harriet was feeling. When you're in your third trimester, your body has changed beyond all recognition and getting dressed in the morning is one of the more *testing* pregnancy nightmares. I mean, are there really any clothes that make you look like you don't have a helium balloon shoved up your top? Self-consciously I adjust the material of my dress that is clinging to my bump and try to breathe in. Just a few more weeks to go, I mutter to myself silently.

I switch my attention back to Harriet. Searching manically through the pile of clothing currently balancing on my left arm, I pulled out a silvery metallic number and handed it over, wincing as I did, as I knew it just wouldn't work over a baby bump.

Let's get one point straight: I am not a stylist. But I do know, having worked with numerous pregnant mothers, what does and doesn't work as maternity fashion. There are certain rules, you see – specific items that you must avoid and others you must embrace.

A dove-grey waterfall cardigan catches my eye on the 'returns' rack at the entrance to the dressing room. I move over and add it to the pile in my arm, thinking how the draped styling will glide over any pregnancy bump, making it invisible – it's exactly the sort of thing Harriet needs.

Edward was occupying himself on the floor by my feet, happily distracted by a basket of Hermès scarves abandoned in the corner. I tried not to notice the rivers of drool he was currently depositing over them and instead concentrated on how content he looked. A contented baby, when out shopping with his mother, is something you rarely come in contact with, so I decided not to interfere and left him to it.

It's only then that I noticed the silence coming from inside the changing room.

'Harriet? Everything OK in there?'

A strangulated sob escaped from the changing room and I jumped slightly, wary that something must be horribly wrong. Harriet was not the sort of woman to cry, let alone in the middle of Selfridges. Cautiously, I moved slowly into the changing room, picking up Edward in my arms as I did so. He also seemed strangely aware that his mother was no longer shouting instructions at us both and her quietness seemed eery.

Another sob, this time louder.

'Harriet . . .?'

Pulling back the curtain to the private 'personal shopping' changing room where she was, I was greeted by a puffy-eyed, tear-stained Harriet, sitting cross-legged in a sea of taffeta (I *think* it might have been the couture size 8 ball gown that she had plucked off a rail back in Ralph Lauren, but I could tell that she had barely been able to get it over her thighs, hence her current position on the floor).

'You must think me so silly.' Harriet had softened in the last couple of moments and I could see a sense of deflation had taken over her usually aggressive demeanour. She reached out her hand to me and I took it, placing Edward down on the floor and sitting next to her, cross-legged. Then she let it all pour out. And I sat, entranced, until she had finished.

'When I was pregnant with Edward, I loved it. I loved the excuse to embrace my body, to wear those horrendous pregnancy jeans with elasticated waists. I would eat those delicious cakes in the Hummingbird Bakery and didn't even worry about stepping out without a patch of make-up on. I was pregnant with a beautiful little baby and that was all that mattered. How I looked was the LAST thing on my mind. All I cared about was having a healthy, happy baby.' She stops and her eyes begin to glisten with tears again. 'Until I saw the photos from the day Edward was born.'

Harriet's eyes glaze over and I saw her shoulders visibly slump. She then looked up at me, straight in the eye.

'You should have seen them, Tiffany. The day Edward was born, Marcus arrived at the hospital with a state-of-the-art camera he had just bought, brimming with excitement. He had spent – oh, I dread to think how much on the most technical, advanced camera there was and he was so excited about capturing photos of Mummy and Baby. I grinned excitedly as he snapped away. Holding up Edward, planting a kiss on his nose. I even told him to get a couple of shots of the hospital room and me in the bed, so that we could remember it. We were both so excited, so pumped by everything.'

She stopped, took a deep breath and then continued.

'But then he showed me the photos. Oh, you wouldn't believe the state of me! There was still blood on my nightdress from the delivery and my eyes – I just looked so exhausted! The nursing bra I had bought online a few weeks before was cutting deep into my breasts, leaving red angry lines, and the nightdress – bought from some random pregnancy shop when we were in Henley for the day – was so revolting and unflattering. My arms flopped out of it and there were colostrum stains where my nipples were. I couldn't have looked uglier.'

'Harriet—'

But she cuts me off before I can continue.

'These were supposed to be images I would treasure forever – that I would frame and put on our dresser in our bedroom. Me, our baby, those first few precious hours. But when I see them now, I just feel sick. Where had the real me gone? Who was this bedraggled, harassed, petrified-looking woman in my place?' A sob escaped her chest and silent tears ran down her face. 'I don't want it to be the same this time, Tiffany,' she whispered. 'I want to be able to have photos of our family of four that I love, where I look at them and think, "Wow, I'm superwoman".'

I placed my hand on hers and stroked it unconsciously. To some, people might conclude that Harriet was being unnecessarily vain, but to the trained eye, I knew it was much more than this. Motherhood is one of the biggest life changes people will ever go through and many, many women lose themselves in it. They lose the person they once were and once the baby is placed on their chest, the old them dissolves forever. It's the one thing I always wish I could warn about and help people with, let them know that it doesn't have to happen to them. I've always said, just because you become a mother, it doesn't mean you have to abandon the 'real you' and it's a motto I live by to this day.

'How would you like to feel when your next baby is born?' I asked softly, careful not to encourage another torrent of tears.

'Like a movie star,' she replied, almost instantaneously.

I felt determination surge through me and reaching for her hand, I pulled her up from the ground, swooping Edward into my free arm as I did so.

'Then we need to get out of here,' I announced, simultaneously typing a text into my phone and smiling as the reply came back instantly. 'We are going to see my friend Francesca. She's a stylist and designer. She's meeting us in 20 minutes.'

The bemused look on Harriet's face made me burst out laughing and I pulled a silly face at Edward in return, getting a giggle from him. 'Come on, superwoman!' I announced, striding towards the exit of the store. 'We are going to turn you into a movie star!'

* * *

Handing me the receipt in a sealed envelope, Francesca raised an eyebrow at me and grinned.

'You nailed it,' she said quietly, taking some more tissue paper and wrapping the final items of clothing neatly before placing them in a bronzed box. We both looked over at Harriet, who was swirling in front of a full-length oval mirror, admiring the way the silk of the dress she was wearing skimmed over her baby bump.

'So, you can definitely have it all ready by October?' I asked again nervously, pointing at the sketches to Francesca's right.

As soon as we had arrived at Francesca's studio in Notting Hill, I had explained what Harriet needed – a maternity wardrobe that would make her feel like the woman she is, not the frumpy pregnant lady she was resigning herself to. Francesca had left us with a pot of herbal tea and enough chocolate chip cookies to gorge ourselves on as she dashed out into the streets of Notting Hill, promising she would return within the hour. On her return, she unloaded bags of clothes filled with wrap dresses, long-line blazers and low, chunky heels.

Prior to Francesca's dash to the shops, she had grilled Harriet on her ideal maternity style and how she felt about her growing bump. They had concluded that Harriet would like some items that could help disguise the bump.

'I hid my second pregnancy for a long time at work, well into my sixth month, by wearing blazers open,' explained Francesca. 'It's how they hide pregnant bellies on TV when the star is pregnant in real life – no one can see your belly in profile.'

We had then discussed the hospital photos and how Harriet would like to feel and look when those first snaps of them as a family of four were taken. Francesca had shushed me whenever I tried to say something, instead concentrating solely on Harriet and what she was saying. As Harriet spoke, Francesca sketched, writing words on a piece of paper and underlining them, before gliding her pencil across the white parchment, drawing as she listened.

'What about something like this?' She held up the paper and Harriet and I both gasped. On it was drawn the most exquisite nightdress. A low V-neck encased with a delicate lace was the focal point for the nightdress, with simple cap sleeves elegantly placed on the shoulders. Francesca had written the words 'Silk' and 'Victorian Lace' next to her sketch and as we looked more closely, she passed swatches of materials over to suggest colour and texture.

'This is a midnight blue,' she said, passing a delicate piece of material to us. 'I know it's advised not to wear white after giving birth because of the potential blood situation . . . I smile at her thankfully – so she had been listening to me when I had explained the 'must-haves' and 'must-nots' earlier. 'But I feel black is just too harsh. So, this deep liquid navy will be perfect. It will bring out the green tones in your eyes.

'Ooh, and this is the best bit,' she squealed excitedly. 'You see these cap sleeves? Well, under here, I will add popper buttons, meaning you can un-pop them to make it easily accessible for breastfeeding.'

I smile, impressed – she really had thought of everything.

Francesca handed me the box of clothes that Harriet had already tried on and approved, then beckoned me towards her so she could whisper something to me:

'The woman who walked in here earlier is completely different to the woman here now. You spotted something in that woman that most people would never have. The fear. The desperation. Lots of people think pregnant women are just full of the joys of spring, but you understand that that's not realistic. Pregnancy and becoming a mother are one of the scariest times of their lives. I have seen so many women who let the old "them" die when they have a baby – and you're proving you're not going to let that happen.'

Chapter 16

The anticipation of birth that engulfed me in the last couple of weeks of my pregnancy was overwhelming. Every time I met with a new pregnant client, I was reminded of how swollen and large my stomach was in comparison and that, very soon, I would be giving birth to the baby that was inside. As I was having a C-section, my experience was going to be very different from many of the birth stories I had heard during my career. For starters, I had an actual date and a time that the baby was going to arrive!

'We'll book you in for the morning slot of the 26th April,' my obstetrician explained calmly as I anxiously ran my hand over my stomach. 'You'll need to get to the hospital at 6am, then we will take you down to theatre at seven, and your baby should be with us by eight.'

I must admit, it all sounded very civilised (at least I didn't have to worry about my water breaking in the middle of the street, or the pain of contractions) but it didn't make it any less scary. The night before, Patrick and I lay in our bed in Chiswick, too nervous with anticipation to even speak. Patrick fiddled with the alarm clock – checking over and over that it was working so that we would wake up in time – and I just lay silently thinking, 'This is it. The last time it's just the two of us . . .' I was petrified, there is no denying it. In the morning, I was going to have my stomach literally sliced open and then everything that I knew about life was going to change. Our 'normal' was going to be blown apart and suddenly we would have to embrace a new role – a role we have had no training for – as parents. Patrick sought out my hand under the covers and squeezed it tightly.

'Are you OK?' he asked, his eyebrows creasing in concern.

'I just can't believe this is it.' My voice sounded quiet and there was an obvious shake to it. 'The next time we are in this bed, we will have a baby lying in the middle of us.'

'And it's going to be amazing.' Patrick finished my sentence for me, and I knew he was right. Life was about to change beyond recognition, but from what I knew from my job, it was going to change in the best possible way.

It was time. The alarm went off at 5am and, as if we were on autopilot, Patrick and I silently gathered up our bags and jumped in the car. As we were driving down Chiswick High Road, completely out of the blue, I burst into hysterical laughter. Patrick turned to me, a confused look on his face.

'We are having a baby today!' I practically yelled. Looking back, I think it must have been the nerves. Adrenaline had hit and the reality of what today meant was really sinking in.

'Well, that's certainly something to celebrate,' Patrick said, a smile spreading over his face. With that, he turned up the song on the radio (George Ezra's 'Budapest' – a song that will continually remind me of the day Rupert was born), and we both sang along at the top of our lungs.

An hour later, I was sitting in my room at Chelsea and Westminster Hospital being prepped for my scheduled C-section, whilst nurses took blood and Patrick changed into his scrubs. Rupert's birth is not a stereotypical birth story. When I was pregnant with him, I agonised for months over how I wanted to give birth. Well-meaning 'friends' suggested that 'natural is by far the best choice for the baby' and various parenting websites pointed to C-sections as 'the thing of the devil' (and should only be done in an absolute emergency). First, I must acknowledge that I was in a fortunate position to be able to have my baby privately, meaning a scheduled C-section was something I could consider. But having that option didn't mean it was an easy decision to make. I, like most mothers out there, spent hours seeking out the opinions of others, hearing about horrific (and not-so-horrific) birth stories and chatting with doctors and midwives about what was best for me and my baby.

In the end, and on the advice of my obstetrician, I decided that an elective C-section was the right choice. My levels of anxiety about giving birth had completely escalated since I found out I was pregnant. At first, like most newly pregnant mothers, I tried to ignore the prospect that this baby had to come out of somewhere unimaginable, but as the months went on, the anxiety levels rose. I would sit awake at 4am, anxiously tapping away at my computer, searching for all the things that could go wrong with a natural birth. I imagined nurses running frantically around my bed, uncontrolled bleeding, the sound of flatlining heart monitors. I didn't want my baby (who in my mind had a fragile little skull) being suctioned or pulled out with full force with a pair of forceps. I didn't want to be rushed into an emergency C-section and then potentially have to make life-saving decisions after hours of labour and no sleep. I didn't want to tear or have the wall between the vagina and anus cut to avoid tearing. Every time I saw a watermelon (yes, I'm back to that watermelon analogy again), I promptly burst into tears and – in my deepest, darkest moment – I even wondered if I actually wanted to be a mummy if it meant I had to give birth. In the end, an elective C-section really was the only option for me.

So, on 26 April 2017, I was walked down to the operating theatre, croc slippers adorning my feet and a surgery gown flapping wildly in the breeze to reveal my (not very pert) bottom. Thankfully, all passers-by were doctors or medical staff who had seen it all before and my naked derrière didn't even manage to raise one questioning eyebrow.

I'd like to say I was brave when it came to the epidural, but I'd be flat out lying. I sobbed like a toddler as the anaesthetist asked me to cuddle a pillow and lean forward so that he could access my back. I knew that, somewhere behind me, a huge needle was being brandished and was about to be inserted into my spine. So, I did what any self-respecting women would do and BEGGED for him to stop. Thankfully, he saw my desperation and instead nodded at the nurse to add a 'gin and tonic' to my cannula. Later, I found out this was morphine to calm me down. Which is probably why Patrick now finds it hysterical to bring up my pre-op revelations of 'I'd like a pink camel as a push present, please'.

Ten minutes later, I was lying on an operating table, knowing my tummy was about to be cut open and a baby would be produced. I suppose you could say it was surreal. But not quite so surreal as having the whole team introduce themselves to me – name and role in the proceedings – and then being asked if I could reciprocate. Not really knowing the etiquette, I launched into a full-blown CV of where I was born, my career history, my first kiss . . . before the anaesthetist calmly placed his hand on my shoulder and whispered, 'Just your name will do.'

Five minutes later, Rupert was pulled from my stomach, fist pumping the air and screaming his tiny lungs out (a good sign, apparently – not just a warning of what was to come). He was placed on my chest; I was wrapped up in tin foil a bit like a marathon runner (the surgery had made my blood pressure drop and I was very cold) and we were wheeled back into our hospital room.

Suddenly, my world (and my heart) had expanded more than I ever thought possible We were a family of three. And life was about to change forever.

At 4am the following morning, with Patrick snoring quietly on the pull-out sofa bed, I leant over Rupert's cot and stroked his tiny thumb.

'I'll make you proud,' I whispered. 'I'll be the best mummy I can ever be for you. That's a promise.'

I'd like to say Rupert opened his eyes and we shared a quiet understanding, but instead he farted and rolled over.

Typical man.

Chapter 17

Rupert is only a few weeks old and I have to face one of the most challenging days of my career to date. I'd promised myself and Patrick that I would take at least a month off work to concentrate on our newborn, but when I got the call from this client I knew I had to help. For once, I had to put my family to one side to help another.

As I push on the nursery door, spider threads catch my face – a sign that no one has been in here yet. Despite a musty smell of abandonment, the nursery smells as a nursery should – a mixture of newly opened cardboard boxes and talcum powder. I look around cautiously and take in the cot, put together by Michelle's husband Henry a few months ago, standing proudly in the corner. A blush-pink cashmere blanket is folded carefully over the rails and a miniature toy bunny rabbit with long muslin ears waits expectantly for its new companion in the middle of the mattress.

A half-opened box sits on top of a dresser and I can see a wooden baby gym poking out of it, with tiny half-moons and stars etched into the wood. To the right of the dresser, in little piles, Michelle had started to fold some of the baby's clothes – perhaps getting them ready to pack into her hospital bag. There is a pink cotton hat folded neatly in half, six baby grows, all with intricate collars and embroidery and tiny pairs of socks, neatly stacked on top of one another in a tower, threatening to tumble.

The sob escapes me before I have even realised. A huge gasping sob that I feel unable to control. Flinching, I hurl my hand towards my mouth, muffling the sounds as much as I can in the fear that Henry might hear me from his office below. Now is not the time to get emotional. I am here to be professional. To carve away at any pain that has been left behind and in some way, try and make it a little bit more bearable.

Michelle had called me a month ago to tell me she was no longer pregnant and that she had had a miscarriage. It was 2am when the mobile by my bed burst into life and I urgently scrambled around, trying to locate it in the dark. Rather than answering the phone to hear hysterical crying, as I would have thought might have happened, Michelle was strangely calm and quiet.

'I know it's late and you must think me mad calling at a time like this, but we have just lost the baby. I wanted to let you know as soon as possible so you didn't waste time doing any more work for us. I know you have lots of other mummies who need your help.'

My initial reaction was to ask her to repeat herself – surely my mind was playing tricks on me in the middle of the night and I had misheard? Only last week we had been unpacking the final bits of baby kit for the nursery. I remember her throaty laugh as she told me in a mock stage whisper that she had already hidden Henry's credit card bill so he didn't freak out at how much money we had spent.

'Well, this baby is going to be the best thing that ever happened to us, so I need to make sure I give her the best, even if it does mean we have to remortgage the house!'

I had smiled along with her, remembering that feeling well.

'Michelle, I'm . . . I'm not sure I . . .'

'Please don't worry about me. About us. We're fine, it's just one of those things.' I could hear her voice cracking as she spoke and I so wanted to reach down the phone line and cradle her breaking heart. 'I just know how tirelessly you have been working, and I keep on thinking about all of those things I asked you to do, and research . . . and I just don't want you to waste your time . . . now that there . . .' A sound like a woman being torn in half rattled down the phone and the sobs followed. 'Now that there is no baby.'

When I started working as a Mummy Concierge, I must admit I was naïve in thinking it would all be baby grows and happiness. Like so many couples desperate to become parents, there is a dark side of pregnancy that rears its ugly head more often than we like to admit. Although 95 per cent of my job is celebrating life and new babies, I'd be lying if I said that there haven't been tears and losses along the way. But Henry and Michelle were the first couple who I had to be brave for.

I had actually been the one to offer to help with the nursery. Paralysed by their own grief at losing their little one so late in their pregnancy, I ended up spending hours on the phone to Michelle, just listening to the grief pour from her like sticky syrup. Rather than researching baby prams and pointing her in the direction of the best baby clothes shops in London, instead I nudged her towards a grief counsellor and suggested that I go to her house and 'undo' her nursery for her.

* * *

Patrick thought I was mad when I announced what I was going to do for Michelle and Henry.

'I'm going over to theirs tomorrow and I'm going to clear out the nursery. They can't bear to even go in the room and I know that unless someone does something about it, that room will stay like that, as a shrine to their unborn baby, for years to come. I have to do something to help.'

Patrick walked towards me slowly and placed his hands on my shoulders, forcing me to look in his eyes.

'Are you sure you can do this?' he asked, quietly. 'You've got a newborn to look after and this isn't on your services list, you know. You don't have to do this.'

But I was resolute. These clients were more than just people I was helping, they were a family – ready to face the world with a loss that would be hard to get over. And I needed to do whatever I could to help them.

Tidying out that nursery was one of the hardest things I have ever done. When people ask me about my job, they laugh and smile as I talk about baby scans, nursery décor and babymoons. It's considered a job of happiness, of new beginnings, new life, and here I was dealing with one side of my job that was the complete opposite.

It took me five solid hours to clear out that nursery. Every baby item that I touched, I felt I needed to respect. I needed to acknowledge that this was intended for a little human being who was no longer able to experience it. Bit by bit, I packed away bags of unused nappies and scribbled 'hospital' on the box in thick black marker pen, so I could take it to the nearest maternity unit as per Michelle's request. I tidied away a baby first aid kit (how cruel that it should even be here, given the circumstances), a pile of bamboo muslins printed with white rabbits holding pink balloons, a teething toy, the BabyBjörn bouncer that Michelle had spent hours choosing.

It was a sobering experience packing away their nursery. My job usually involved lots of 'to-do' lists – neatly typed-out inventories of 'things to buy, things to do, things to prepare', followed by little square boxes that parents take great joy in ticking off. But today, it was as though I was doing my job in reverse: all the kit was here, the wallpaper covered in little boats with blue sails was up, the cot was assembled, and I was taking it apart. Crossing off 'ticked' items, peeling off wallpaper, unscrewing and dismantling the cot for the baby.

I'd be lying if I said that that evening, when back at home, I didn't march straight into Rupert's nursery and pull him from his cot, hugging him so tightly that Patrick had to take him from me – worried that I would squeeze him too hard. When something is taken away from someone, with no warning, it really does make you realise how precious the things you have in your life are. I learnt a huge lesson that day – never take anything for granted. That night, I slept on the floor of Rupert's nursery and nothing was going to move me.

I just needed to be close to my little boy.

PART SIX

FOURTH TRIMESTER

Chapter 18

When I was pregnant with Rupert, people often asked me if I was going to breastfeed and I nodded along, mumbling something along the lines of, 'Sure, I'll give it a try, but if it doesn't work for me then I will happily switch to formula.' Even when I was pregnant, I had an unease around breastfeeding. Other mummies seemed intent on sticking to 'breast is best' (God, how I hate that saying), whereas I already had anxieties building up around it. How do you actually breastfeed? Was it going to hurt? How did I feel about getting my boobs out in public? But there was also something else there, right in the back of my mind, that I was never willing to admit at the time. (And even find hard to admit now, for the fear of being judged.) The thought of having a baby sucking my nipple made me feel queasy – I just didn't feel comfortable.

I pushed that thought away, knowing 'it wasn't the way a mother should think', whilst trying to bolster up the jovial confidence that I saw every other breastfeeding mum on Instagram portray. If they could do it, so could I. 'Stop being such a wimp' was my daily mantra.

When Rupert was born, within seconds the midwife asked me if I wanted to 'put him on my breast'. I nodded, not really allowing myself the chance to contemplate if I did actually want to do it. Embarrassed, I pulled apart my hospital gown and clumsily tried to put Rupert near my nipple. I felt hot, flustered and completely out of my comfort zone. I even asked Patrick 'not to watch' as it felt so uncomfortable to me – a small human was about to suckle on my nipple and I was about to produce milk. It was very unnerving to me.

I sobbed through the multiple feeds that came after. I vividly recall my sister and mother coming to meet Rupert at the hospital and they sat in the room with me, my obstetrician at my side, all trying to encourage me to feed my son. Patrick had gone for a walk so it was just us four women in the room, each of them making suggestions on how to hold the baby, one how I should be sitting, asking if the colostrum was seeping from my nipples. I felt like a caged animal. I didn't want this, it didn't feel natural to me. Instead, I felt like I was on show, proving to everyone in the room that I was already failing as a mother despite Rupert only being two hours old.

When we got home from the hospital three days later, I took to my bed and heeded the advice of my doctor to try and rest as much as possible so as to recover from my C-section surgery. Days started to merge into each other with one startling factor that filled me with fear: every three hours, I was going to have to feed Rupert.

I wasn't going to admit my fear to anyone – I didn't want to give anyone a reason to think I wasn't being the best mummy I could be. So, feeds became my nemesis. Whenever Patrick handed me Rupert, saying, 'He's hungry,' I would plaster a smile on my face and retreat into the nursery, where behind closed doors, I would sob uncontrollably as Rupert fed. As night-time approached, I tried to gee myself up for what lay ahead. I would download episodes of comedy stand-up routines in the hope that something – *anything* – would make me smile during those night-time feeds. I would always retreat to Rupert's nursery to feed him – even in the dead of night when it would have been easier to pull him next to me into our bed and feed him lying on my side. The nursery was my 'sanctuary'. It was the place where I could close the door, block out the outside world and sob freely. It was the place where I could dig my nails into the palms of my hand as Rupert drank hungrily, the place where I looked at my little boy in the dim 3am light and thought, *Can I really love you if you make me this sad?*

A few days after Rupert was born, Patrick's parents flew over from Ireland to meet him. That morning, I woke up a bundle of nerves – feeling as if I was an actress about to go on stage. I remember standing in our tiny en-suite bathroom in our home, smearing tinted moisturiser over my face, adding more and more, hoping it might disguise the sheer panic that was etched on there. I stood in front of my wardrobe and picked out a bright pink sweater – hoping this might distract from the way my hands shook every time I was handed Rupert. Then I heard his parents arrive and the gentle, soft coos as they were introduced to Rupert downstairs. I took a deep breath, plastered on a smile and descended the stairs. I knew I didn't look right. I knew I wasn't looking like the adoring, contented mother I should be – but I was going to try my hardest to put on an act.

No one could know how I was really feeling.

I knew something was really wrong with the way I was feeling. It was much, much more than 'baby blues'. Holding my baby and feeling like I wanted to put him in his cot and run away was not normal – I knew that too. But I was scared. So incredibly scared of admitting the truth to myself or anyone else.

It's hard to admit that. *Very* hard. And the reason? I always thought I was just born to be a mummy. I just presumed it would all come easily and that I would excel in looking after a little baby. Never for one minute did I anticipate that, for several weeks, I might hold my newborn 'bundle of joy' and just be overcome with a sense of panic. I never thought that the cracked nipples, extreme tiredness and the baby's endless cries could actually bring me to my knees. Also, breastfeeding was hard. Harder than I could ever have imagined. And I had no idea what was about to come . . .

My breastfeeding experience wasn't what I wanted it to be. And looking back, it probably would have been better had I never done it, but I did still learn a lot and for that, I'm really grateful. So here are my own top ten truths about breastfeeding.

Top ten truths about breastfeeding

1. **You'll probably have a lazy boob.** Like it or not, one boob WILL decide it just can't be arsed. And as a result (let's call it competitive boob syndrome), the OTHER boob will decide it wants to supply as much milk as humanely possible ALL IN ONE GO. Yup, you'll have one A* boob and one D- in the achievement stakes. As a result, one boob is very likely to be triple the size of the other. (See truth 4 for more info.)

2. **Nursing covers are a scam.** I bought every one. LITER-ALLY. EVERY. ONE. And what did I end up using? A muslin tied in a knot around my neck. Why? Because muslins are so much EASIER. Nursing covers might 'claim' to be 'the essential for discreet feeding' but I have yet to meet one that actually works. By the time you have worked out how to get it around your neck, slipped your arm through the right hole and positioned your wriggling baby underneath, you might as well have screamed out to everyone in the coffee shop, 'I'M GET-TING MY BOOB OUT NOW AND ATTEMPTING TO HIDE IT UNDER THIS MONSTROUSLY UGLY NURSING COVER!'

3. **You can eat, and eat, and eat . . . and not put on any weight.** DISCLAIMER: As soon as you STOP breastfeeding, then you continue to eat, eat, eat and the weight just piles itself back on. (Yup, there's that honesty I was talking about!)

4. **You will end up waterboarding your baby.** Nipples leak, and squirt and produce a HUGE AMOUNT OF MILK AT THE EXACT TIME YOU DON'T WANT THEM TO. Usually when your baby is positioned underneath, smiling and waiting for his breakfast. And what happens? As your 'let down' occurs, it is essentially like 'letting down' Niagara Falls. In your baby's face.

5. **You have to rejig your wardrobe – goodbye tight-fitting and high-neck tops.** It's all about easy boob access. That's literally ALL you will care about when breast-feeding. Gone are the tight-fitting Joseph cashmeres or the Whistles high-neck winter polos you were desperate to wear. In their place? Anything with zips, buttons or (dare we admit it) one of those 'Ooh, look, I can lift this up and my boob falls out the bottom!' tops that are 'on trend' in maternity clothes outlets.

6. **Your boobs will quite literally change size every day.** Want to have DD boobs? I can give you that on a Monday. Fancy testing out a left 34B and a right 36C? Yup, scheduled in for Tuesday. Boobs filled with milk

equals boobs of continual different sizes. Just get used to it.

7. **Hello there, drips, stains and leaks.** All hail the sanitary towel for the nipple (aka breast pads). Without these genius inventions you will constantly walk around with milk stains on your T-shirts (not quite the look you were going for, right?). Also, when you are breastfeeding, one boob will *always* leak whilst your baby feeds off the other so you essentially end up sitting in a pool of milk. My advice? Make sure you have plenty of muslins to hand.

8. **You WILL wake up in a wet patch.** Oh yes, that milk likes to leak at the most inconvenient times. Such as when you've just nodded off to sleep (having spent four hours trying to get the baby to sleep!). Suddenly, mid-dream, you're woken by the strange sensation that you're lying in a sticky, sickly wet patch. And you are . . . Yup, that will be your milk (and dare I say it, the smell is also AW-FUL!). Change those sheets immediately!

9. **It can make you feel isolated.** If you're not one of those 'I love breastfeeding, it's so natural and lovely' type mothers then (ahem, this is so NOT me), this one is for you. I HATED breastfeeding, particularly in public, which meant whenever my baby needed feeding, I whisked myself upstairs (or at times to the disabled

toilets) and breastfed there ... alone and isolated. The solution? Download a good box set and set aside breastfeeding time as YOUR time. It's not often you have an excuse to sit by yourself and watch *Made in Chelsea* on repeat (I mean, David Attenborough, um, David Attenborough . . .).

10. **You will probably end up expressing in the disabled toilet or a Portaloo.** Fancy a nice big glass of wine or a trip to a festival? Yup, that Portaloo or disabled toilet is your new best friend. I'm being serious.

Chapter 19

Before Rupert was born, I confidently told anyone who would listen that I wasn't putting any pressure on myself whatsoever as to what I was going to be like as a mother. I nodded along with my NCT group when we all chatted about 'giving breastfeeding a try, but not stressing if it didn't work' and happily researched baby-wearing, co-sleeping and other parenting trends, internally giving myself permission to give or not give anything a try. I wanted to be the epitome of a 'chilled mama' – not letting my baby rule my life but also not letting any decisions I made about parenthood cause me any drama. I adopted the mantra 'you do you' and repeated this to anyone who would listen – I'll do me, and you do you. NO judgement.

So, when I brought Rupert home from hospital, I stuck by my promise and gave breastfeeding a go. Subconsciously, I noticed the praise I was receiving from everyone around me when I told them. Friends messaged to say: 'Yay, breast is best!' Magazine articles online virtually clapped their hands at me when I joined the ranks of breastfeeding mums. My health visitor practically jumped up and down when I lied and said breastfeeding was going well (but did sneer in the direction of a random formula bottle we had on the shelf, asking why I needed that if it was all going so well).

That formula bottle was both torment and relief. On days (which were becoming more and more regular) when I was sitting downstairs, idling watching catch-up episodes of *Entourage*, silently willing Rupert to stop feeding, I would glance at that bottle and think, *Maybe I should just stop. Maybe formula feeding isn't so bad?* But there were other moments, usually those dark moments in the middle of the night, when I'd think about switching to formula and hear all the voices in my head: *Don't do it. It's bad for the baby. You'll be a bad mum if you don't breastfeed. You'll be a failure. Everyone will judge you.*

At first, I didn't realise I was seriously ill with postnatal depression. Since Rupert was born, I awaited the onslaught of 'the baby blues', which your doctor and NCT class warn you about. On day five, I sobbed (completely textbook) and then laughed with Patrick afterwards that the baby blues were incoming.

A week later, I was still crying. My days were spent with Rupert on my breast, feeding him on demand and hating every minute of it. With this, came the tears. The complete onslaught of negative emotions that I didn't know how I would survive another day. The exhaustion was overwhelming – I couldn't sleep because I was worrying too much about the following day. *What if someone suggested going out for a walk with Rupert and he needed feeding?*

What if I couldn't get him out of his pram? What if he started screaming and won't stop?

Panicked, I took out a notebook and started writing a list of all the things that could go wrong. By day seven, I had filled 13 pages with worries.

At the time, it did not feel like postnatal depression so much as a months-long panic attack.

A month later, and I was delirious with exhaustion after two hours trying to settle my miserable, screaming baby. He just wouldn't sleep and I had tried everything. I knew that if I fed him, he would probably settle, but the thought of putting him to my breast filled me with such an innate fear that I couldn't face it. I thought about putting him down, walking out the front door and never coming back. Five minutes later, I was tearfully apologising to my son, nuzzling his neck, promising I'd never leave him.

There were moments when I would stare in the mirror and not recognise who I was. I had many moments when I would wonder what it would be like to fall down the stairs, because if I got hurt, I wouldn't have to take care of the baby and maybe, just maybe, I could get some sleep.

Whilst I was crumbling inside, I didn't want anyone to know. By admitting how I was feeling, I felt like I was admitting that I was a bad mother. Every other woman out there seemed to be nailing motherhood and there I was, failing at even the most basic bits.

I also started to notice various family members looking nervous around me and this sunk me even lower into a pit of gloom. I didn't want them to see that I had failed. They had to think I was a super mum. Suddenly, I felt like I was being a burden to everyone. Every time Patrick came into our room, he was greeted with a sobbing mess of a wife. When my sister called to chat, I could barely form a sentence, too worried was I that I'd start crying and never stop.

I was tired of being a burden on everyone too. I didn't want people whispering about me behind my back. I saw the way friends and family were looking at me with disappointment in their eyes and I wanted them to think I was happy and enjoying motherhood. So, I had a brilliant idea – I would simply pretend to be OK. I would put my drama degree to good use and just play a role. If I couldn't be the perfect mother in real life, I could at least pretend to be one.

My NCT class were arriving at my house one day for a baby massage class which I had arranged with a local baby expert – so desperate was I to fill my days and have people around me. Being alone in the home was something I was getting increasingly incapable of doing. The fear that vibrated through my body when Patrick closed the front door behind him in the morning as he set off to work on occasion had me rushing to the bathroom upstairs, Rupert hanging off my hip, whilst I silently vomited into the loo. So, I began to do what I always did when I felt stressed: *I planned*. I sent out messages to my NCT group suggesting various baby-related classes and activities, I made list upon list of baby things we still needed to buy (convincing myself that 'if we just had this', life would become easier).

Opening the door to be greeted by a clatter of smiling new mummies, their tiny newborns cuddled to their chests in baby slings or sleeping peacefully in various brands of prams, I felt the sensation in the pit of my stomach that was becoming more regular: fear. All of them looked so pulled together, so capable. They laughed and smiled and joked as they picked their babies up and placed them gently on baby mats in front of them.

I held back for a few moments, under the pretence of putting coats in the spare bedroom, and let the tears flow freely. Rupert lay in my arms, his big grey eyes staring up at me as tears dripped onto his face. Then, as quickly as I had started crying, I stopped, pulled myself up off the bed, straightened my top and pushed my chin out. Walking past the ornate mirror in the corridor at the stop of the stairs, I inhaled deeply and then plastered on a smile. It was the fakest smile I had ever seen, but it would be good enough to fool them – the last thing I wanted was for them to think I was failing.

Twenty minutes later and seven babies had been massaged and sung to in my living room. I can't tell you anything else about that class apart from the fact that I remember watching the women around me sing and smile and laugh. It was as though I was trapped in a horror movie. Everything seemed to be going in slow motion. The smiles on their faces got wider and more terrifying, the music from the instructor's iPhone louder and more tinny with every song. I was getting more and more anxious: 'They're looking at me, they're thinking I'm a terrible mother, I *am* a terrible mother . . .' Before I knew what I was doing, I'd jumped up from the floor and sprinted upstairs, back into the safety of my bedroom. Rupert had been left, abandoned on his playmat.

His mother had failed him again.

I'd never heard of 'a mother's mask' before, but up in that bedroom I started frantically googling. Meanwhile, I could hear the concerned voices of the NCT girls downstairs. Someone asked if they should 'take Rupert upstairs to be with me'. This was followed by a silence which you know means people are talking about you in hushed whispers.

So, I did it again. I stood up, I rubbed the leaky mascara from under my eyes and smiled at myself in the mirror. That's when I clocked: I was putting on my motherhood mask. The fake smile, the upbeat vocabulary – it was all a mask to hide behind so that no one could see the person I actually was – an awful mother to my baby boy. Then I walked back downstairs, scooped Rupert up in my arms, smothered him with kisses and then apologetically (and casually) explained away my recent exit due to 'exhaustion – I was awake from 1–6am this morning!' This of course was met with numerous sets of shoulders dropping in relief, a communal exhale. It was as though I had given permission to every mother in that room not to worry about me.

'I didn't sleep last night either,' they all exclaimed, relieved that they were now in the realm of being able to impart advice. 'Have you tried feeding less/more/a white noise machine/a night nurse?' Nobody actually looked at me properly and realised, 'She needs help, this isn't normal'. And I suppose, because of that, I continued to convince myself too.

This was just motherhood. This was just what life was going to be like from now on . . .

But there were some days where you just don't want to wear that mask, so you stay in the house. I cried constantly and became overwhelmed by the simplest tasks, such as entertaining Rupert when he was awake or putting his baby clothes in the wash. Everything felt like an uphill struggle and even the most routine day-to-day activities felt like an impossible challenge.

Whilst Rupert slept, I would sit at our kitchen table writing routine upon routine, detailing minute by minute what I should be doing each day. I suppose a part of me felt that by doing this my days would be filled, so I would have less time to 'just be'. Because 'just being' was the scariest part of my life. It would be when I would sit, often in a dark room, sobs heaving out of my body like there was no end. Or I would stare at my small son sleeping calmly in his cot and think, *Are you OK? What if I just walked away and left you? Maybe you'd be better/happier without me around.* If postnatal depression had one distinguishing characteristic, it would be that I felt totally like my mind and body were not in my control. My thought patterns were totally irrational and I felt smothered and heavy, like I couldn't breathe.

In those moments when I attempted to get out of the house (advice that was constantly imparted on me by family members who were convinced I just had baby blues), I would look down at Rupert in his pram, tell him 'I love you' and in the same breath hear myself apologising to him that he'd got me for his mother, how awful I was and that I hoped one day he'd have someone better. I knew, in those raw moments, that something was wrong – that it wasn't normal to feel this way, but like wrapping myself up in cotton wool, I refused to face the truth and battled on, my mummy mask plastered on my face.

There is a certain cruelty that comes with being a mother who is suffering from postnatal depression: you want so badly to be happy and in control, you want to be enjoying the moment, because everyone keeps telling you that this is the most special time in your life. Instead, you're a crying, confused mess.

The day it all came to a head was when my mother came to visit us. I was so looking forward to her arrival, but for all the wrong reasons: once she was here I could hand the baby over. I could feign 'exhaustion' and ask if it was OK if I went and slept. And then I could shut myself away in our room and hope that I would never wake up.

True to form, she arrived at our home, arms filled with gifts for the baby and a car boot bursting with home-cooked food, which she swiftly placed in our freezer. She took a crying Rupert from my arms and within seconds, he had stopped, entranced by this new, magical woman who seemed so at ease and happy to be around him.

Patrick arrived an hour later and I watched him and my mother chat easily, my husband laughing, and regaling her with stories of what Rupert had done that day. I remember sitting there – completely numb – and realising all these milestones that Rupert had met – a squeeze of a thumb, a smile – hadn't even registered with me. Here was my husband in complete marvel at our little boy and I felt nothing. I constantly compared myself to Patrick, who seemed to take to this whole parenting lark so naturally that I looked woeful in comparison – he was being an incredible father, whereas I was failing incredibly, it seemed.

I walked up the stairs, not feeling anything, and opened the door to my room. I clocked the Moses basket next to our bed, my 'breastfeeding timetable' taped to the wall, the breast pump taunting me from the bedside table. My breath started to shorten, each one feeling as though someone had their hands around my neck. An intense heat travelled up from my toes, to my legs, to my torso and I started to shake. I heard footsteps running up the stairs and it was only then that I realised an animalistic noise was coming from my mouth: I was screaming. Fear, terror and sheer panic were making their way out of my body in one long scream.

I don't remember much after that apart from running to our en-suite bathroom and locking myself inside. Patrick and my mother were outside, banging on the door, begging me to confirm I was OK. I sat on the floor, hands over my ears, willing it all to stop. Willing life to go back to what it was like before Rupert, before this complete mess I had made of being a mum.

It was only when I realised Patrick was trying to bash down the door – he later confirmed that he was concerned I was going to do something awful – that I slowly slid back the lock and collapsed in my mother's arms. It was one of those moments in life that I will never forget. Here I was, at the lowest ebb of my life, desperately needing my mother yet the thing that was killing me was being a mother myself.

* * *

The next few days blurred into one. Patrick called various doctors and I had numerous initial phone chats with perinatal specialists. Our health visitor came to see me, her face ashen with concern as she made me fill in a postnatal depression form. I had to answer questions with a rating of 1–10 (10 being suicidal).

I scored 7 and above for every answer.

My family stepped in as soon as they realised the severity of the situation. My mother didn't leave our house after that fateful evening and silently slipped into a role where she cooked us meals, hugged me when I needed it and updated my father on how I was doing.

I remember spotting a stream of texts on her phone between her and my dad. I had picked it up, thinking it was mine and was hit with a deep sadness when I saw the text: 'How is our little girl doing today?' My mum had replied saying that I was trying to get better and that I ate a piece of toast (followed by a thumbs-up sign.) She signed off, 'Our little girl will be fine. We will make sure she is.'

That's when I realised that even though I was in my thirties, I was still their 'little girl' – that parental love is all-encompassing, and they would do anything to make me better. I remember feeling a flash of hope then.

I must – and would feel like this – about Rupert. I must get better.

As we slowly went through the motions of getting me help, Patrick was my rock. He never once questioned me, never once confirmed my fears that I was a bad mother. Instead, he took it on his shoulders to make me better. He googled article after article about postnatal depression and wrote notes as he did so, comforting me with recovery statistics at the end of the day as he handed me a cup of a hot chocolate ('Chocolate solves everything' used to be my other motto).

He also spoke to a close friend of his from university who he knew had suffered postnatal depression, and she gave him a list of books, blogs and experts I could research to make me feel better. But the main thing he did, which I honestly think saved me, was to encourage me to stop breastfeeding.

Having my husband actually say the words, 'Why don't we switch to formula?' was like a huge, suffocating weight being lifted from the fog in my brain. It was as though I was suddenly being given permission to do – if I honestly admitted it – what I had been wanting to do from day one. Postnatal depression is triggered by different things for different mothers – tiredness, a traumatic birth – but for me, the trigger was 100 per cent breastfeeding.

I can be completely honest about how it made me feel (and please don't judge me for this – I understand the benefits, but I also understand every mother must do what works for her): I felt like a cow being milked. It's that simple. I didn't have any other excuse for hating breastfeeding. I was lucky to have enough milk. Rupert fed well and apart from one bout of mastitis (an inflammation of breast tissue that antibiotics sorted out quickly), the mechanics of breastfeeding was going well. But I wasn't used to using this part of my body in this way. I wasn't used to having a small human suckle and squeeze and essentially 'milk' me. It wasn't the romantic, wonderful image that so many other mothers describe it as. To me, it was a form of torture. Something that made my toes curl and made me feel less like a woman. I hated the thought of breastfeeding in public, of breastfeeding in front of my family. I wasn't one of those women who could happily whip out a boob and continue a conversation – I wish I was, but it wasn't me.

I must admit, I'm scared writing this, because even though I have made peace with my decision to bottle-feed

Rupert, I know some people will still judge me. I know they will whisper how I 'didn't give my baby what's best for him' and that people will argue that I should have kept trying for longer – that it would have got better. But it's important to me that I'm honest. And it's also important to live by the mantra that I always tell the mummies I work with: You do YOU.

Without a happy 'you', you won't be the best mummy you can be.

I want to make sure that anyone reading this doesn't think I'm saying that breastfeeding might cause you postnatal depression. That is not the case at all. For me, it was the trigger, but that is for my own personal reason that I discussed with a psychiatrist and dealt with. I work with, and have many friends who are breastfeeding mothers, and who genuinely love every moment of it. All I want to make clear is that, like every woman is different (some enjoy running marathons, others can speak multiple languages), every mother is different too. We all have our different ways of doing things, our triggers that make motherhood hard and our unique motherhood moments that make us feel like superheroes. Just because one mother has nailed motherhood in one way, it doesn't mean you can't nail it in another.

* * *

The first day I gave Rupert formula, I completely tortured myself. My mum and Patrick were both with me and we decided to try and make it a casual 'normal' thing to do by heading into Chiswick on a hot, sunny day to sit outside in the beautiful gardens of one of my favourite restaurants. The plan was I would nip into Boots to buy Rupert a bottle of ready-made formula and then we would all sit outside in the sunshine, whilst I fed my little boy and the three of us celebrated with a G and T.

The reality was awful. As I walked down the road pushing Rupert in his pram, my mother and Patrick chatting happily behind me, a sense of dread started to build up with every step I took. I watched other mothers walk by, presuming they knew that I was about to do the worst thing ever to my baby and give him formula. As I got closer and closer to Boots, my heart started to palpitate in my chest and my hands grew hot with sweat. I looked down at Rupert, happily playing with a grey muslin in his bassinet and apologised silently to him.

Patrick and my mum went on to secure a table at the restaurant and left me to tackle the shop by myself. I have since asked why they did this – why they didn't come with me to support me? – and they insisted they thought me doing it by myself was for the best. They had hoped I would realise no one was judging, no one even cared what I had in my shopping bag, and that I would emerge from the shop feeling more confident.

That wasn't the case. As I walked into the shop, I rapidly scanned the names above the aisle until I saw the baby section. I pushed Rupert towards it in slow motion until we were facing a shelf full of baby formula. I felt a hot trickle of sweat run down my back and grabbed the first ready-made bottle I could see, swiftly covering it in my basket with an array of dummies, bibs and nappies that I didn't need – I suppose I was trying to hide my shame, praying no other mother would see what was in my basket and judge me.

When I eventually sat down in the garden of the restaurant, my face streaked with hot, angry tears, I clumsily opened the bottle and shoved it in Rupert s mouth, desperate to get this public feed over and done with. It was the wrong thing to do: he started crying as milk spluttered all over his face and in a moment of desperation, I pulled at my T-shirt, my body heaving with tears as I tried to get my boobs out of my bra – insisting it was better to feed him that way.

In the end, Patrick took Rupert off me, wiped down his face and slowly put the formula bottle to his mouth. Without a minute's hesitation, Rupert happily latched onto the bottle and guzzled away. Minutes later, he was fast asleep in a milk-induced nap and looked as happy as anything.

Looking back, I don't know what caused me to have the meltdown, but what it did do was confirm to me that I still needed help. When I got home that afternoon, I immediately called a perinatal psychologist. After my first session just a few days later, I agreed to start taking anti-depressants. Within a week, I had stopped crying every day – something I hadn't even realised I'd been doing – and the cloud lifted.

To say I lost myself that first year is no exaggeration. I don't recognise my face when I look at photos; all I see is my false smile and a tired, desperate look behind my eyes. Like many people, my first year of motherhood was undoubtedly the toughest time of my life. I think it's safe to say that I was traumatised afterwards and it took me a long time to feel like me again.

For me, the antidepressants, support from my family and weekly chats with my psychiatrist helped tremendously, but there's no denying it took a huge toll on my husband, too, watching his wife, his best friend, fall apart before his eyes, turning into someone he didn't recognise. There were times when I caught Patrick sitting in the kitchen, Rupert asleep on his knees, just staring into space. He looked exhausted and beaten. Something I have learnt is that postnatal depression doesn't just affect the person dealing with it – it affects the family around you too – which tells me there is even more reason to get help as soon as you can.

Sometimes clients will ask me if I have ever had experience with postnatal depression. I have always been very open about what I went through and there are times when I will chat to mummies about it when I feel like I can see they are slipping into something similar. I'm no doctor, but I honestly feel that once you have been through it yourself, it's easier to spot in someone else – it's the look in their face that confirms it, the sheer panic behind dull, unseeing eyes.

A few years ago, I did have to deal with postnatal depression face on again, but not from one of my mummy clients. When my phone rang at 6am one day, I immediately assumed it must be one of my clients going into labour with last-minute questions about their hospital bag, but when I answered, I was greeted by a man's voice.

I could immediately sense he felt scared.

'I don't know if you're the right person to talk to, but my wife is always singing your praises and I didn't know where else to turn,' he mumbled. He had a well-educated accent – the type you might expect from someone who went to Eton. I nodded into the phone and gently asked how I could help. His words came thick and fast.

'My son was born a few months ago. The birth was pretty traumatic – my wife ended up being rushed into surgery and lost lots of blood, but she and the baby were fine.' He stopped and stammered, and I could sense tears were falling at the other end of the phone. 'When the midwife handed me my son, I felt nothing. It was like a stranger coming into my life. I didn't get that rush of love. My wife struggled when we came home so I had to put on a brave face and make sure everything was going along smoothly. I even extended my paternity leave so I could be at home and help with the baby and look after my wife. It meant I wasn't paid for a few months so that was a bit of added stress.'

Listening to this stranger talk, I felt an overwhelming sense of wanting to help. I knew where he was going with this, I understood his pain.

'Anyway, it all came to a head last night – I was changing my son's nappy and he wee'd all over me. Rather than laugh it off, I felt an intense feeling of failure. I couldn't do this anymore. I ran downstairs and into my garden and just screamed.'

'Have you spoken to your doctor about this?' I asked gently. I was no expert but to me the signs of hopelessness that he was feeling and the lack of control sounded just like I had felt in my darkest times.

'That's the thing. I've read a lot online and I suppose the reason I've called you is because I think I know what it is, if it's even possible? I sat through those NCT classes when they spoke about how women can get postnatal depression, but to me, it seems that's what I've got. Is that even possible?'

I'll never forget that conversation and it sparked in me something that I still try to encourage today. A lot of ante-natal classes talk lots about how mothers might feel after the birth of their little ones, but they rarely touch on the partners. Fathers – despite this being the 21st century – are still expected to take everything in their stride when it comes to having a baby. Their role is to look after their new baby, their wife, finances, but dads need support too.

Chapter 20

When Rupert was just six weeks old, I remember looking idly on the calendar on our wall and realising that it was the wedding of two of our closest friends who we had met in Australia many years ago. To those of you thinking 'How can you forget a wedding?', I promise you, in those first few weeks with a newborn, it's easy to forget anything.

Panicked, Patrick and I ran around our home desperately trying to find the wedding invite (it was stuck on the fridge hidden behind a 'breastfeeding schedule for Rupert' routine I had pinned there a few days before). The wedding was in Suffolk and thankfully at the bottom of the invite in small letters were the words, 'Babes in arms welcome'. In a complete daze, Patrick and I managed to confirm the hotel we were staying at, pressed 'buy' on a silver teapot on the wedding list and started to gather together everything we might need for a night's stay away with a newborn.

'This should be easy!' Patrick joked, as I tried on yet another dress which didn't fit before throwing it on the ground in a huff. 'Isn't this part of your job? Telling people how to travel with a newborn?'

'We will have to get a travel cot and make sure we have enough nappies, and baby grows . . . What if he gets sick whilst we are away? We don't know a doctor in Suffolk. What if he needs feeding during the church service? And his naps – how will his naps work? We need to make sure he naps otherwise—'

Patrick cut me off before I could finish by simply placing a finger over my quivering lips.

'We can do this,' he said softly. 'Sure, we are new to this, but it's not going to be the hardest thing we ever have to go to. It's a wedding. With friends. And they know we have a newborn. We will figure it out, I promise.'

That night, I lay in bed and I didn't feel so certain. Rupert was asleep on my tummy and I was desperately trying to write a list of all the things we needed for the weekend away in order to attend this wedding. So far, the list totalled 78 things.

Opening up my phone and being careful to quickly turn the bright screen away from Rupert's face, I typed into Google: 'Wedding essentials with a newborn'. Hundreds of websites appeared before my eyes and I rapidly clicked through each one, adding items I hadn't thought about to my list as I read. At 4am that day, I had had exactly ten minutes' sleep and there were 123 things on my list.

How the hell were we going to do this?

* * *

Four days later and we arrived (two hours late!) to the wedding. Trying to be organised, I had woken at 6am in order to leave enough time to get everything sorted and in the car before our 10am departure. I had embraced the morning with an attitude of 'I can do anything' and had been happily loading up the car (note to reader: NOT advised if you have just had a C-section) since 6.35am. I had my list with everything I needed now neatly printed out on A4 paper and was contentedly crossing everything off one by one as I loaded it all into the car.

The meltdown happened approximately 43 minutes later. With Patrick still snoring happily in bed, Rupert had since woken and I was attempting to feed him whilst simultaneously pouring out enough cat food for our cat Rooski to keep her content whilst we were away. The inevitable happened: the bag of cat food overflowed, biscuits spilled everywhere, Rupert stared yelling (probably because in my shock at the cat food explosion I had moved quickly and stopped feeding). Trying desperately to placate Rupert, I spun around quickly and the bottles of breast milk – which I had spent days before expressing as though my life depended on it – fell to the floor with a crash. And that's when the tears started (me, not Rupert). At this stage I was attempting combi-feeding, to rid myself of the guilt of stopping breastfeeding, and these were the last bottles of breast milk that I had.

It didn't go unnoticed that I was literally crying over spilt milk, but as any mum who has endured hours of being strapped to a breast pump in order to have some milk as a backup knows, this is possibly the worst thing that can happen. Not only had all my hard work literally gone to waste, but in my desire to be organised, I had already got dressed ino my grey silk dress for the wedding and now it was stained all the way down the front with stale-smelling milk.

An hour later, our bedroom looked like the Apocalypse. Every item of clothing I had ever bought was strewn all over the wooden floorboards and there I was, in the middle of the room, sobbing again. Patrick was at his wits' end.

'What's happened? Where's Rupert? What HAVE you got on?' He came and pulled at the fuchsia pink pashmina which was hanging from my shoulders and (not so subtly) trying to disguise the 'far too small' floral minidress I had bought from Topshop about 12 years ago.

Yup, it certainly wasn't my best look.

'Rupert's in the washing machine. I'm having a meltdown and I'm wearing this because nothing else fits me and I hate my body and I'm not going to the wedding!' I wailed dramatically and waited for Patrick to sort everything.

'Rupert's in the washing machine?' A horrified look passed across his face.

'No, not IN the washing machine . . .' I didn't have time to explain as Patrick dashed downstairs and returned ten minutes later with a contented-looking Rupert in his arms.

'I thought you'd lost the plot and put Rupert in for a spin cycle!'

I laughed despite myself (and just in case you're wondering, I had actually put Rupert in his baby bouncer in front of the washing machine – a brilliant hack that I now tell all of my clients, as babies love the noise and motion of watching the water go around). As I pulled myself up off the floor, Patrick grimaced in my direction again and handed Rupert over to me.

'You're not really going to wear that, are you?' he said, nodding in the direction of my floral ensemble. At that point, as if comic timing couldn't happen more accurately, Rupert promptly vomited all over my dress. In the immortal words of eighties pop band D:Ream: 'Things can only get better'.

Thankfully, despite the unprecedented start to the day, the wedding went like a dream. We crept into the back of the church just as they announced that the bride and groom could kiss and Rupert congratulated them in the only way babies can, by farting loudly. The rest of the day zoomed past in the blink of an eye. Everyone wanted to hold and cuddle Rupert and for the first time in a long time, I had a couple of minutes child-free to chat to friends I hadn't seen in years and enjoy a sneaky glass of champagne. As if determined to prove he was a good baby, Rupert slept soundly throughout the wedding breakfast. We had brought along a small Moses basket that sat safely next to our table in the corner of the barn where the wedding was taking place and he didn't even wake when a six-piece Australian band started blaring out nineties chart hits. Looking back, I feel sad that I spent those four days in the run-up to the wedding in such a state. I did what I presume most new mummies do and conjured up every possible nightmare scenario that might have happened (poo explosions over the bride's dress, hysterical crying during the father-of-the-bride's speech, an inability to even put the baby down for five minutes so as to have a wee), but as is usually the case, none of them actually happened.

When Patrick and I flopped into bed that night (at 9pm, I must admit, as it was already way past Rupert's bedtime), we lay in the darkness and just squeezed each other's hands. We didn't have to say anything, but the unspoken words were clear: We had done it. We had survived. We were superhuman.

The next day, I was woken by a new client who (talk about fate!) had just been invited to a wedding and was panicking because her baby would only be a few months old. I smiled happily down the phone, reassuring her as I spoke that she would be fine and even sending her a WhatsApp photo of Rupert, the day before, being cooed over by a clatter of bridesmaids. As I finished the conversation, I reached for my laptop (Rupert and Patrick were still happily dozing) and made a note of some tips I could share with any clients who might be attending a wedding with a newborn. I still use this list to this day:

How to survive a wedding with a newborn

1. **Bring as many muslins as humanely possible.** I packed ten for this wedding. TEN! And you know what? I wish I'd packed double the amount – it's simply amazing how many go missing/get thrown up on (and that's even before you get to the church!).

2. **If you want to drink, bring your breast pump.** Everyone knows weddings = champagne, so if, like me, you want to indulge in some bubbles, then a pump will be your new best friend. There were three fellow pumpers at the wedding – all covering up with shawls as the pump did its thing – and then happily quaffing back champagne. 'Pump and Dump' is an expression that will become an integral part of your vocabulary if you like a drink or two!

3. **Make a pact with your other half that you will share the childcare duties.** The last thing you want at a wedding is to be holding the baby for the entirety so, before you head to the church, agree that you will take it in turns to share the baby load. Patrick and I had determined this the previous day, with me looking after Rupert during the reception (so he could catch up with old school friends) whilst he manned him during the wedding breakfast so

I could eat (it's amazing how difficult eating a full meal becomes when you are a mother).

4. **Get some baby ear defenders.** Unfortunately, I hadn't thought about this in advance. Once the wedding breakfast was over, the party started and the band started playing in full force. Whilst we were happily dancing away, with Rupert in-between us, it was then that I noticed every other baby in the vicinity was wearing small fluorescent ear defenders to block out the sound of the music (and presumably not damage their little eardrums!). I felt like an awful mother as the realisation dawned that I was exposing my baby to live guitar, drums and a sax at a deafening volume, which led to me disappearing outside and ferociously typing 'baby ear defenders' into an Amazon order straight away.

5. **At the church, make sure you can sit somewhere with an easy escape route.** At the end of the aisle or the back of the church is perfect. After all, the last thing you want is for your baby to start screaming blue murder just when the priest asks if anyone objects to the marriage going ahead!

6. **Stock up on breast pads.** There's nothing worse than rocking a new dress and then noticing you have wet milk patches where your boobs are. It's always a good idea to have a pashmina or shawl with you at a wedding. Not

only does it double up as a breastfeeding shawl, but you can also drape it around you to disguise any milk stains!

7. **Palm your baby off to anyone and everyone!** The great thing about weddings is that almost EVERYONE (and I mean everyone) will want to hold your baby. We had a completely fabulous moment when one of our friends from Australia insisted that she take the baby for a walk around the estate grounds to give us a break. If only I'd had a camera to capture her, slightly tipsy, pushing the pram across the lawn with one hand, an espresso martini in the other!

8. **Understand that there will be unglamorous moments.** Mid-wedding breakfast (and due to an intense dislike of breastfeeding in public), I found myself traipsing across the car park (in the POURING rain) to get into the back seat of our car in order to feed Rupert. Whilst everyone else was partying the day away, I was boob out in the back of a BMW – oh, the glamour!

Chapter 21

It was 11am on a Monday and my working day was commencing with a swim in an infinity pool in Ibiza. The translucent turquoise of the pool water rolled over my shoulders as the sun warmed my back and I did lap after lap. As I pushed my head up out of the water to catch my breath, I could see the unending expanse of the Mediterranean Sea below me, the craggy shelves of the cliffs on either side melting into it.

The flight over had been bittersweet. I was so excited about my work enabling me to travel abroad, but at the same time I was desperately worried about leaving Rupert, who was only a few months old. Granted, he was being looked after by my family and Patrick, but I was already missing those captured smiles in the middle of the day, or the odd gurgle that I had been so used to witnessing, day in, day out. But work called and as it was only a few days away, I knew it was something both Rupert and I could survive.

When I took on this job, I had a sense it was going to be glamorous. I had been working with Paulina, a new mummy of a six-week-old, since she was eight months pregnant. During her last trimester, I had done bits and bobs for her, such as finding her an antenatal class and packing her hospital bag, but I knew that she wanted to use my services more once the baby arrived. So, when I received a phone call from her, telling me she had booked me a flight to Ibiza, it didn't really come as much of a shock.

Heaving myself out of the pool, I reached for my bottle-green sarong that I'd discarded on the floor 40 minutes earlier and drew my wet hair off my face. That was exactly what I needed – a relaxing swim before the chaos started. Feeling refreshed, with the outside thermometer showing 33 degrees, I made my way up the cobbled pathway towards the Ibizan villa that was to be my home for the next four days.

When I had arrived that morning, sweating profusely under all my luggage and desperately trying to remember some of my schoolgirl Spanish so as to direct the taxi driver, I landed on the villa doorstep with a thump (the luggage, not me!) and an overwhelming sense of awe.

I don't think I had ever seen anywhere as beautiful.

Paulina's holiday rental was just exquisite. The rustic stone walls, terracotta roof tiles and clouds of pink blossoms heralded it as a traditional finca at heart, but as I stepped inside, I could see that a modern style had been added to the home so as to satisfy more elite and stylish occupants. The entrance hall was seashell-smooth and decorated in shades of cream, sage and coral. Walking into the main open-plan living room, I could see flashes of Ikat painting, blue-painted wooden beams and quirky sculptures (the focal point was a larger-than-life alabaster face). A pillow-piled, two-corner sofa ran along the perimeter of the room's three walls, taking in the views of the Mediterranean from the floor-to-ceiling sliding doors opposite. As I stepped out onto the main terrace, I was lavished with an unending sight of blue sea, dotted with four elegant wooden sailing boats, their flags dancing in the wind. To the left, I could see some tiny turquoise and white fisherman's cottages, wrapped in fuchsia bougainvillea. I made a note to go for a walk later that evening and try to find the hidden beach that Paulina had insisted I visit, 'when all the work is done'.

Bounding upstairs to check out my bedroom (Paulina had given me a floorplan of the villa so I knew exactly who would be staying where and which room needed to be filled with what baby equipment), I threw open my bedroom doors to reveal a soothing balance of white linens and cream stone. An oak four-poster bed sat serenely in the middle of the room and to the left, an en-suite bathroom was separated from the sleeping area by a sliding door, which pulled back to reveal a monsoon shower, freestanding bath and a plethora of cosy-looking towels and bathrobes. But what really caught my attention were the two Juliet balconies and the huge, breezy private roof terrace flanked by cappuccino and blush pink sun loungers.

Goodness! If this was a 'staff' room, I couldn't even begin to imagine what the main suite must look like.

I had presumed I would be the only person in the villa at the time. However, on arrival, I was greeted by Javier, Paulina's private chef, who announced the day's menu of finca-fresh omelettes, traditional paellas and spicy grilled fish. I noticed that the dining-room table had been set for one and Javier explained that Paulina had booked him for the three days I was there so that I didn't have to worry about 'getting to grips with the kitchen'. Paulina, her husband and baby were arriving in three days' time, which meant I had enough time to complete everything she had asked me to do before her arrival. My purpose on this trip was to completely babyproof the entire villa, something which in theory sounds pretty simple. Teamed with Paulina's specific demands, though, it was certainly going to be an all-encompassing task.

On my arrival at the airport, I had already checked that the car that had been booked to collect Paulina, and Charlie had the exact same brand of baby car seat as Paulina had back in the UK. I had also delivered a bag of 'car journey essentials' – complete with toys for the baby, nappies, wet wipes, a changing mat, baby sun cream and a hat – to the chauffeur and insisted everything needed to be within arm's reach as soon as the family were enclosed in the car. Paulina had been very concerned about the two-hour ride from the airport to the villa ('What if the baby doesn't stop crying or I need to change her nappy?') so I had reassured her by getting together a travel SOS kit for their journey.

Before I left the UK, I had made sure Paulina had a bag for the plane (which I packed myself and delivered to her door on my way to the airport), carefully laden with ready-made formula, bottles, dummies, soft baby books and various muslins to wrap, wipe and snuggle with. I had also convinced a new travel brand to loan us a travel mattress especially for newborns, which unfolds safely onto a parent's lap whilst on a plane, just in case the request for a baby basinet made to the airline was not met (for those of you who don't know, if you are flying with a baby then you can request a seat at the front of the plane, which will have a fold-down basinet for your little one to sleep in).

I had also made a note on my iPhone to call Paulina the morning she was due to travel, to remind her to pick up the 'mummy bag' I had packed for her and left in the nursery. This bag, amongst other things, had a spare pair of jeans and top. Paulina had shown me her travelling outfit a few weeks earlier, exclaiming, 'You have to look fabulous when entering Ibiza!' It consisted of a white pair of designer jeans and a linen shirt in the palest blue. I had seen far too many baby poo explosions mid-air not to know that if you choose to wear white when travelling, then you should always travel with a spare outfit, so a spare pair of jeans and T-shirt had been folded neatly into her 'mummy bag' complete with other essentials such as paracetamol, face moisturiser and an iPad (in case she got stuck under a sleeping baby).

Abandoning my towel on the nearest sun lounger, I ran upstairs and changed into some linen shorts and a T-shirt before attacking my to-do list. Throughout the morning, various deliveries had been arriving at the villa, complete with harassed-looking Spanish delivery men, who made no attempt to disguise the fact they would rather be eating tapas in a beach bar than helping me unload various baby kit. Hoping they might offer to help the obviously frazzled Englishwoman to unpack the boxes and then remove them, they had instead grunted at me when I asked them to wait and proceeded to smoke about 20 Marlboro Lights on the terrace whilst watching me do all of the hard work.

Thankfully, and allowing myself a swim as a reward, I had eventually unpacked all of the boxes and they had removed them from the villa, meaning I was now faced with a living room full of every sort of baby paraphernalia you could imagine. Pushing my sunglasses up on my head, I set to work, putting everything into relevant piles: three highchairs, travel cot, sheets, toys, swimming essentials, play gyms, Moses baskets, baby monitors . . .

You might notice that all of these items are plurals. That's because Paulina had insisted we needed one of everything for each room. Every bedroom was to be graced with a Moses basket just in case the baby slept better in different rooms throughout the day. We had baby monitors which could be positioned in bedrooms, on the terrace and down by the pool, and highchairs that would sit at the indoor table in the dining room, one for the outside terrace by the pool and another for the BBQ area.

In between the unpacking, I regularly checked my phone for updates on Rupert. Patrick was incredible at sending me video snippets of their day and it made me feel less far away from them both. There was one box that I was extremely excited to unpack, which Paulina had shipped over a week earlier. It was full of the most beautiful baby outfits you could imagine: hand-embroidered bonnets, linen baby grows, tiny smock dresses with daisies handstitched onto them. Reaching into the box, I pulled out numerous newborn vests, hats, bloomers and swimming costumes, stroking them softly and imagining how gorgeous Paulina's baby would look in them. I had thought ahead and, in my own suitcase, packed 50 baby hangers, knowing the hangers in the wardrobes would be far too big for newborn outfits. Gathering the clothes up into my arms, I hurried upstairs to the nursery, which I had started working on the night before. I had assembled a cot and added a few toys to make it look exactly like Paulina's nursery at home – noting that I still had to source some frames for the prints that Paulina had ordered (again, exact replicas of the ones at home) so that the baby would not feel 'confused by her new room'.

Paulina had asked me to assemble a holiday wardrobe for the baby and to put together outfits for each day of their trip, so 14 outfits, each with their own variables dependent on the weather and if they might take the baby into the pool. For the next two hours, I sat on the nursery floor and put together baby outfit after baby outfit, matching cornflower blue smocks with pale linen bloomers and swimsuits with hooded towels.

Folding up another newborn cardigan and spritzing the now-immaculate wardrobe with lavender spray, I smiled to myself.

Life really was pretty good at the moment.

PART SEVEN

HONEY, I WANT MY OLD LIFE BACK

Chapter 22

The first time I had a call from a celebrity, I was in New York on a Christmas mini break with Patrick and Rupert. We were walking through Central Park, Rupert snuggled up in his pram and Patrick and I bundled up in so many scarves and sweaters that you could barely see our faces. It had been snowing solidly for the last three hours and having been cooped up in our minuscule hotel room (New York hotels are not known for their spaciousness), we had decided to venture out and see if we could rent one of those horse and carriages to take around the park. I was just pulling myself up into one of the carriages (and desperately trying to avoid eye contact with the horse pulling it – horses make me nervous) when my phone let off a shrill beep, alerting me to an incoming call.

Flustered – I had one leg in the carriage and the other desperately trying not to slip on the icy concrete below – I pulled it out of my coat pocket and distractedly answered.

'Yes, can I help?'

'I'd like to speak to Tiffany, please.'

A clipped British accent echoed down the phoneline and I knew immediately that I was speaking to someone important – there was just something about the way she said my name that oozed authority. I gave Patrick a panicked look, whilst trying desperately to pull my scarf down away from my ears so I could hear properly. Thankfully, Rupert, currently in Patrick's arms, was far too entranced by the horses to demand any attention.

'Speaking. How can I help?'

The horse had started to amble its way along the path, pulling us along behind him and I relaxed back into the carriage, Rupert bouncing around on his daddy's knee, completely excited by this new experience. I couldn't help but notice, however, that Patrick was huffing beside me – I'd promised this break away would also be a break from work – but I concluded that I'd placate him with a beer and ice skating around the Rockefeller Center later that evening.

'I'm Sandra Halford, the PA to Mr Matthew Aisles, and we would like to use your services.'

I balked slightly and my face must have given me away as Patrick raised his eyebrows in my direction, obviously wanting to know what was going on.

Matthew Aisles is a very famous singer who found his fame in the boy band days but has since extended his career into acting. He had been with his girlfriend since they were teenagers and a few years ago, they got married and had a baby shortly afterwards.

The cold New York wind was biting into my knuckles as I held the phone up close to my face, wishing the sounds of the city around me would melt into nothing so

I could make sure I took in every word this PA was saying clearly.

'Mr and Mrs Aisles have a new baby, Jacob, and a toddler, Coconut.' I clamped my hand over my mouth to stifle my giggles – why do celebrities have to give their children such ridiculous names? 'They are in dire need of a new nanny – someone who can start within the next month – but are really struggling to find someone suitable. But, here's the catch . . .'

The horse had stopped outside a pretty restaurant in the middle of the park and Patrick had jumped out and was paying the driver. I flapped my hand at him, not knowing what to do – should I stay in the carriage and finish the conversation or jump out and hope the PA didn't hear the snort of the horse in the background? I opted for the latter.

'Right, and the catch is?'

Walking away from the restaurant, I found an upturned tree trunk and plonked my bottom down on it. It was icy cold but at that moment I didn't care, I just wanted to get to the bottom of this phone call. I smiled across at Rupert – who was bouncing towards a puddle, much to Patrick's horror – and turned my attention back to the phone call.

'Well, we have all tried to find someone suitable, but whatever nanny we have interviewed doesn't seem to understand the – how shall I put it? – highs and lows of working for a celebrity.' The voice on the other end sighed and I imagined her raising her eyebrows to the ceiling. 'The job is obviously very different from that of a normal nanny and that's why we need you.'

'Oh, no, I'm so sorry. I can't help, I'm not actually a nanny.'

She cut me off before I could continue. 'We know that – Mr Aisles saw an article about you, that's why he asked me to contact you. We want you to come here, meet Coconut and see what a day in the life of a nanny for the Aisles would be like. Then, once you have experienced it, we want you to find us the best nanny for the job.'

I scrunched my nose up as she continued speaking, trying to understand exactly what it was she wanted from me.

'So, forgive me for asking, but you essentially want me to test out the nanny job and then find someone who will fit it?'

'Exactly.'

I heard a thud on the other end of the phone line and could only imagine her thumping her desk with her fist in satisfaction.

By Jove, she's got it!

'Listen, I'll email all the details over now but we would need you here no later than Thursday. Coconut has a lot going on that day so it will be the perfect way for you to see what an average day in the life of a celebrity toddler is like.' She laughed – a thick, cackling laugh that made me shiver. With that, the phone went dead and at the same time an email pinged into my inbox. It was from Sandra – I'll give it to her, she must be the world's most organised PA.

Skim reading it quickly whilst I walked towards where Patrick and Rupert were playing in the snow, I realised that this was one job opportunity I couldn't turn down. It might be slightly out of my comfort zone, but as far as I was concerned, what better way to help a family find their ideal nanny than to step into the nanny's shoes?

* * *

Later that evening, Rupert was asleep in his cot and Patrick had gone up to the hotel's rooftop swimming pool for a swim (despite the snow still falling). I had taken the opportunity to curl up by the fire in our room and call a couple of celebrity nannies I already knew, just to understand a bit more about their jobs. I always believe that if you are going to throw yourself in at the deep end, the best way to be prepared is to 'be prepared', so I needed to know what I was letting myself in for. The first call I made was to an ex-maternity nurse based in New York, who I once met at a baby conference. Screeching down the phone when she realised I was local, she promptly insisted she come and meet me at my hotel so she could tell me all the juicy details face to face.

Patrick, refreshed after his swim, agreed to keep an eye on Rupert, and half an hour later I was in the downstairs bar of the hotel as Christine launched herself into the room, enveloping me in a huge hug and charming the waiter to bring her a cup of hot milk.

'It must be working with babies for so long,' she said, her thick Birmingham accent oozing out of her. 'I just can't get enough of the stuff! Reminds me of being at home on a winter's night and having a mug of milk before bed.'

Christine was dressed in her usual get-up of thick, elasticated stripy trousers and a bright orange coat. To say she didn't let fashion bother her would be an understatement – this woman was purely about comfort and wasn't ashamed to admit it.

'When you've worked as a maternity nurse for as long as I have, all style goes out the window!' She laughed as she shrugged off her coat to reveal a knitted, stripy rainbow-coloured sweater. 'What's the point of dressing up if a baby is just going to poo or puke up all over you? You've got to be comfortable in my job, that's what I tell you. Comfort is everything.'

Christine's love for the children she works with never ceases to amaze me. She has worked as a maternity nurse for over 40 years and she can honestly remember the name of every baby she has ever cared for – 'They all carve a special place in my heart,' I remember her saying when we first met. 'To forget one of them would be like forgetting a member of my family.'

'Well, where do I start?' Christine had pulled her stripy legs up under her and warmed her hands before the fire. 'Some of the celebrity jobs were certainly the more interesting positions I have taken.'

I shifted forward in my seat, desperate to take in every detail.

'There was one celebrity mummy I worked for who hired an interior designer for her children's bedrooms . . .'

Now I had worked with lots of parents who would like designers for nurseries and children's rooms – maybe celebrities weren't actually much different from us mere mortals. But a wicked smile spread across Christine's plump cheeks.

'She had three children at the time – a two-year-old, a four-year-old and a seven-year-old. I had just been hired as their nanny – it was one of the first jobs I took after nanny college – and she told me she wanted to give them all a gift as a surprise for being good at school.' I nodded along as Christine continued. 'Now, we're not talking a new Peppa Pig DVD or a football.' She laughed loudly and shook her head in amazement. 'She asked me to source an interior designer to turn each bedroom into an "immersive experience" – those were her exact words.'

I shook my head in wonder: *what the hell did that mean?*

'Well, exactly – I had no idea what she was going on about either, but I googled a couple of interior designers and got them to present us with some ideas.'

I made a note in my notebook – nanny duties could extend to sourcing interior designers – then put down my pen to continue listening.

'In the end, we settled on one woman – she turned the four-year-old's bedroom into an airport – he had a bed made to look like a helicopter, with controls and everything!'

Christine picked up her phone and started scrolling through before showing me a photo of the most exquisite toddler bedroom I have ever seen. The bed was indeed in the shape of helicopter, complete with blue and white exterior lighting and a stunning array of gadgets and extraordinary features such as a personalised dashboard with a joystick, speed dial, clock, radio with adjoining speaker. 'The bed alone cost £35,000. For a bed! Can you believe it?'

I really couldn't, but she hadn't finished yet. 'The seven-year-old had a room that was designed to look like a castle – it had a huge turret in the middle with the bed on top and a magnificent "moat feature" which circled it. It was amazing how they did it – they attached some lights to the ceiling so that when the main lights in the room were off, the moat glistened and looked like real water. I think that's what the mum must have meant by an "immersive" room.'

I shook my head in amazement and jotted down a few more notes. 'So, what do you think my day will be like with the Aisles?' I asked.

She scanned the email Sandra had sent me earlier and then reached over to take my hands.

'I'm not going to lie to you, Tiffany. This is probably going to be one of the toughest jobs of your life . . .'

Chapter 23

A week later and I'm back in the UK, standing in the hallway of a magnificent mansion in Chelsea. I had walked around this area a lot when I lived in London and always marvelled at the sheer size and glamour of the houses.

'You must be Tiffany – I'm Angela, one of the PAs. If you can come this way . . .'

Angela ushers me into an expansive living room with a domed ceiling. Light is spilling through it, creating rainbow-infused shadows on the oak-panelled floor. The room is completely spotless. There is one large window overlooking a small but immaculate garden and three white leather sofas surrounded by vase upon vase of white hydrangeas. I subtly look over my shoulder to see if any toddler toys have been stashed away in a corner in a mad hurry to make the room look tidy, but I can't see a single flash of colour or an arm of a teddy bear anywhere.

'This is the adults' living room,' explains Angela, as if reading my thoughts. 'Coconut and Jacob are not allowed in here on any occasion.' She hands me a folder and flicks it open, pointing at a room plan of the house, which has various red crosses throughout it. 'These rooms are all child-free, so both the children and nanny are never to be seen in any of these locations.'

I squint at the piece of paper and notice there is a red cross through the garden area – surely not?

Again, Angela appears to read my mind before I can question anything.

'The children are allowed access to the second garden, which is to the left of the house down the back stairs. It's far more child-friendly and their parents like to be able to relax in the formal garden without the noise of the children disturbing them.'

I nod solemnly, trying to convey understanding, although to me this is one of the most surreal things I have ever heard.

What parent doesn't want to hear their children doing roly polys in the garden or squealing with laughter?

At that moment, there is a brief knock at the door and a petite woman, dressed in a normal maid's outfit, enters.

'This is Consuela,' Angela gestures towards her and Consuela bows – actually bows! – at me. 'The new nanny will have to liaise with her daily about the menu for the children. Are you taking notes?' She looks at me pointedly and I whip out my notebook and scribble down: Menu with Consuela.

'Today is going to work like this . . .' Angela sweeps around the room, puffing up hydrangeas whilst simultaneously glancing at her BlackBerry. 'You will step into the role of the nanny and deal with Coconut and Jacob for the day. The idea is, you get a feel for the job, so when you start interviewing nannies for us, you can tell them what we expect from them.' I nod in what I hope is a silent, but understanding manner. I'm suddenly feeling very nervous – I'm certainly not a nanny and just hope I can pull this off. Again, Angela seems to sense my concerns: 'You will have our other nanny with you at all times, of course. Usually, we have three nannies on the go at any given time so there is one per child and one as a backup.'

A backup nanny? Wow, I must admit I had never heard of that before.

'So, just to be clear . . . The job you want me to recruit for is the nanny for Coconut?'

'Yes. She is nearly four. Starts school in September so we need a nanny who can entertain her until then.' She beckons towards the file I'm holding. 'Everything you need to know is in there. Why don't I leave you for a bit to go over it all and then I'll introduce you to Mr and Mrs Aisles and the children?'

With that, she has swept out of the room, leaving a trail of Hermès perfume in her wake, and I'm left alone with the file aptly labelled in type on the front: 'Nanny Rules and Job Credentials'. I flip it open and see a list of 'Must-haves' on the first page. Oh, my goodness, this was going to be one tough job to fill! Here's a cut-down example of some of the credentials listed:

- **15/20 plus years' experience (must be a career nanny).**
  OK, so that shouldn't be too hard to find. Career nannies are the sort of nannies who really devote everything

to their job. They have usually trained at Chiltern or Norland (some of the most prestigious establishments). A few nannies I have met in the past spring to mind and I make a note of their names next to this.

- **Fluent in at least three languages (must be willing to speak English in the morning and another language in the afternoon – French or Japanese preferred).** I gulp loudly. I've heard of families wanting bilingual nannies before, but have never seen such exact instructions about what language they should be speaking at what time of the day.

- **Willing to sign attached Non-Disclosure Agreement.** There is a pink Post-it note stuck on the page, directing me to the back of the file, where a ten-page legal document sits. I flick through briefly – I've never seen a Non-Disclosure this long – and decide to tackle the details on this when I'm back home that evening.

- **Must have proficient abilities in skiing, swimming and horse riding.**

- **Ideally plays one musical instrument to a very high standard.**

- **Self-defence training preferred – although we are willing to pay for lessons, if need be.**

- **Degree in Child Psychology a bonus.**

I run my eyes down the rest of the list, the butterflies in my stomach getting greater at each bullet point. There's no doubt about it, this family really are looking for Mary

Poppins. The funny thing is, I'm not nervous about finding them the ideal nanny – there are lots of nannies out there who work their backsides off to be the best and I'm pretty certain I'll be able to find at least three or four I can send this family's way. The nerves in my stomach are there because, today, I have to BE this nanny.

What am I going to do at 2pm when they expect me to flick over to another language? I barely passed my French GCSE . . .

Before I have another moment to worry, the door is flung open and a little girl, her head almost obscured by a halo of wild white curls, runs over to me and flings herself into my arms. She smells of peaches and plasticine.

'Are you my new nanny?' she asks, her blue innocent eyes looking up at me in wonder. 'Mummy said you're going to look after me today, but I want you to stay forever.'

She envelops me in a huge hug and I smile openly – what a gorgeous little girl!

'Page 7, clause 6a: No cuddling the children. I suggest you spend some more time reading the rules.'

A tall, thin woman who reminds me slightly of Skeletor from the He-Man movies strides into the room and removes who I presume must be Coconut from my lap. 'Mrs Aisles prefers her nannies to touch the children as little as possible so they don't become too attached.' She proffers a hand to me and I stand up to shake it. 'I'm Mila, Jacob's primary nanny. Are you ready to go? We are due at Baby Pilates in ten minutes.'

Coconut has positioned herself behind my back, out of sight of Mila, and I feel her little hand reach into mine as Mila storms out of the door. I squeeze it gently and she squeezes back. Immediately, I feel a bond with this little girl. It's as though we have a secret code already – I'll look after you, you look after me.

Coconut leads me out of the room and points to a red duffel coat and patent plum shoes in the corridor. 'You have to put those on me,' she whispers. 'And don't forget to collect my snack from Consuela in the kitchen – Mummy likes us to be vegan on a Monday.'

'Oh, thank you, Coconut . . .' I bend down to her level and speak softly. 'But I think I have to wait here to meet your mummy and daddy. Angela said—'

'Oh no, Mummy and Daddy won't meet you yet,' Coconut explains eloquently. 'They only meet new staff members once they have been approved by Angela and then Derek – he's our butler.'

I feel a shadow fall over us and I look up to see Mila, her tall, skeletal frame looming over us.

'Come, Coconut.' She points a finger in Coconut's direction and then flicks it towards me. 'And you . . . Mrs Aisles has just texted to say she will meet with you later this afternoon. For now, you are the nanny.'

* * *

Moments later, I am sitting between an excited Coconut and Jacob, being driven by their distinguished chauffeur Manock to their Pilates lesson. Coconut hasn't stopped talking.

'Jacob is only six months, but he loves Pilates, doesn't he, Mila? Mummy says all babies must do Pilates by the time they are one. I started when I was three months, didn't I, Mila? Mummy said I was the youngest in the class, but also the best. Mummy said I could put my toes in my mouth before any of the other babies . . .'

I smile encouragingly at Coconut as she talks, trying to make a mental note of what life must be like for these children on a daily basis. Mila, in the meantime, is talking away loudly on her mobile in the front seat – she has barely looked at me or said one word since we left.

This is going to be a long day.

Chapter 24

'Change of plan!' Mila barks at no one in particular. 'Pilates has been cancelled – let's head over to Christian's as he's holding an impromptu play date.'

Coconut squeals in excitement at my side and the verbal diarrhoea starts again. 'I love Christian. He's my godfather, but Mummy said he doesn't believe in God. Mummy says that doesn't matter, though, because godfathers are really only there to give you presents. Christian gave me a rocking horse for my first birthday and I fell off it and bumped my head, didn't I, Mila?' She cranes her neck to get Mila's attention in the front seat, but Mila is too engrossed in her BlackBerry to notice.

Minutes later, the car pulls up at a huge white gate which has a security guard outside. Manock rolls down his window and the security guard clocks Mila and ushers us through. The house is very similar to the Aisles' house and benefits from being set discreetly behind a high wall, offering a feeling of privacy. The road it's on looks like it has jumped out of a Mary Poppins' movie, with pink cherry trees lining the pavements. I notice the street sign says 'The Boltons' and make a mental note to google the area when I get home.

If ever I win the lottery, this is where I would want to live.

Coconut clambers out of the car the second we pull up and I busy myself getting Jacob out of his car seat. Mila snatches him from me, reminding me *she* is his nanny, and then ushers me to follow Coconut's retreating back. I gather up what I presume must be Coconut's backpack (scooping up a Barbie doll, which has made a bid for freedom) and shove it back in the bag before following her down the long marble corridor of the house and into a huge living room.

To say I'm star-struck is an understatement. The room is filled with about six other children, ranging from babies to five-year-olds, but it's the adults who leave me speechless. Whilst the children play with various toys and musical instruments on the living-room floor, lounging on sofas are a plethora of famous musicians, actors and TV presenters, all drinking coffee and talking loudly. I can feel a red-hot blush rise on my face as a very famous rock star raises his coffee mug in my direction and smiles. A man, who I presume must be Christian, envelops Mila in a stiff hug and then saunters over to me, a leather jacket strewn casually over his shoulder:

'You must be the new nanny. Welcome!'

He has a thick LA drawl and something clicks in my brain – I think he was the star of an interior design show I watched briefly on my trip to New York.

'She's the Mummy Concierge,' Mila is quick to answer before I get a chance.

'The other nannies are in the conservatory,' he says, glancing back over his shoulder. 'We are going to start the music class in a bit, but for now, why don't you mingle with the others and grab a decaf?'

I look over towards Coconut and see she is happily constructing a wooden puzzle with another little boy who I think was in *Hello!* magazine a few weeks ago. She looks happy and calm so I put her rucksack down on the floor near her and make my way to where I presume the conservatory is, following the laughter. As I put my hand on the door and gently push it open the laughter stops and five terrified-looking faces greet me.

'Oh goodness, we thought you were Christian and that you'd been eavesdropping!' says one stunning girl with wild red hair. She walks towards me, smiling. 'We were just having a gossip about the latest celeb demands. You must be Coconut's new nanny, right? I'm sure you have some stories . . .'

She offers me a spot on a tall bar stool propped up against the breakfast bar and I try to climb up onto it as elegantly as I can, smiling as I do so. One of the other nannies jumps up and offers to make me a coffee and I'm handed a box of biscuits, which it seems everyone is gorging themselves on. As I listen to the excited chatter happening around me, I can feel the stress seep out of me – these girls are much more my type of people.

A petite blonde with her hair in braids sits cross-legged on a stool to my right and plays with the laces on her baseball boots as she listens. I guess she's in her early twenties and just as I'm about to start up a conversation, she jumps up off the stool and starts rummaging around in a bag by her feet.

'Hudson needs his jabs,' she explains to the other nannies as an alarm sounds on her Apple watch. 'He's diabetic,' she adds, looking over in my direction. 'Thankfully, I was a paediatric nurse before this job, so it doesn't faze me.'

She produces a little medical kit and ambles towards the door, calling Hudson's name as she does so. A little boy of about four years old emerges, dressed in a knight's helmet and brandishing a wooden sword, and his nanny expertly lifts up his shirt and pushes what looks like a pen into his tummy. He doesn't even flinch, instead waving his sword in the direction of the living room and runs off to join his friends.

'He's a trooper,' the nanny, whose name I now know is Anna, explains as she notices what must be a very impressed look on my face. 'His parents couldn't bear to inject the insulin themselves – his mum hates needles – so when they hired me, the fact I'm also a nurse really helped.'

For the next 15 minutes, I sit and chat with the other nannies, listening intently as they exchange horror stories about life as a celebrity nanny. Despite the fact they all look young, I very quickly learn that these nannies probably have more experience than most. Three of them are bilingual, one has just graduated from Oxford University and another used to ski for England. Alexa, nanny to two-year-old Tallulah and eight-year-old Scarlett, chats about some of the previous jobs she has had with other celebrity parents.

'The dad was a nightmare,' she reveals, raising her eyebrows as she speaks. 'He couldn't keep his penis in his pants and the press inevitably found out about it.' I listen open-mouthed as she talks. 'Every time a story broke, I'd get a phone call ordering me to pack up the kids and drive to their secret holiday house before the paparazzi arrived. I had to teach the children hand gestures they could use to alert me if they saw a photographer.'

'Oh, that's nothing,' says Nikki, an American nanny who is lounging on the sofa, drinking a green smoothie. 'My previous employer had a thing about how we had to walk in case we got snapped by the paps. I had to walk in formation with her entire entourage. Her friends, assistants, bodyguards and nannies had to fan out behind her, like geese in a flying V formation.'

The other nannies collapse in hysterics and I can feel competitiveness surge through the room.

'You think that's bad?' says a tall black girl, twirling her dreadlocks. 'A mum I once worked for has a rule about her kids "walking lightly". I wasn't expected to just enforce this rule, I had to follow it as well. God forbid if I made any noise walking to the bathroom!'

I look around in amazement at the girls surrounding me. I'd often heard stories of what it was like working as a celebrity nanny, but usually dismissed them as likely to have been exaggerated. Sitting here now, I could tell stories like this were just part and parcel of the job though.

'So, tell me . . .' I pick this moment to enquire about what I should be looking for in a nanny for the Aisles. 'What was their last nanny like and why did she leave? Any tips on the sort of person I should be looking for?'

Anna hands me another biscuit – how do these nannies stay so thin? – and then reaches into her bag. She looks over at the other nannies and they all nod. Solemnly, she hands me a small notebook. 'So, here's a bit of a guide,' she says whilst I gently flick through the pages. 'When you've worked as a celebrity nanny for a while, you learn a few things and this is something we always pass on to others who get into our circle. Just so that they know what to expect.'

The first couple of pages are bullet-pointed notes – I see words such as 'self-defence' and 'paparazzi' and can't wait to read it all properly.

'But when it comes to the Aisles, I actually think they are one of the best families to work for.'

'Yeah,' Alexa butts in. 'I knew their old nanny Lorna and she said the parents are actually quite down to earth – once you see past all the celeb stuff – but it's the staff who cause problems. Some of the staff have been working for them for years and they don't relish new members coming into the household. I think that Mila woman can be a bit tricky . . .' She grimaces as she says this and I nod, completely understanding – Mila certainly hadn't come across as that 'encouraging' when I first met her.

'Lorna left because she couldn't deal with the paparazzi element,' Alexa went on to explain. 'She absolutely loved

Coconut and Jacob – she was in pieces when she had to leave them – but the paps had started to hound her and followed them everywhere. She was worried about the safety of the children.'

I frown, but lean forward, keen to hear more.

'There was one pap in particular who took a dislike to Lorna – probably because she was very good at shielding the kids from the photographers – so he started up a rumour about her having an affair with Mr Aisles. It was completely untrue, but she began to receive hate mail, and one day someone even smeared her car with dog poo.'

'Oh, my goodness, that's horrific!' My hand flies to my mouth as the other nannies look on complacently.

'But the Aisles really are a lovely family,' Anna continues. 'They love their children so much and would do anything for them. I honestly think when you're trying to find them a nanny, you want to find someone who already understands the life of a celebrity nanny and who has a thick skin when it comes to the paparazzi bullshit you have to deal with.'

The other nannies nod in agreement. 'But they also need to be able to love those kids like their own. Their mum travels a lot for work so isn't around all the time and the dad, although quite hands-on when he can be, is often working most weekends. So, you need to find a surrogate mummy, someone who the kids can completely fall in love with.'

I nod and make a mental note in my head – nanny must be kind.

'And a degree in Lego construction might help too!' laughs Alexa. 'Either that or a magical ability to make everything perfect in every way!'

We all raise our coffee mugs and cheers to that – I think this might be one of my most difficult jobs yet.

Ten minutes later and the nannies' coffee break is officially over as we are all bombarded by 12 over-excited toddlers announcing that music class is about to start. Self-consciously, I tidy up Coconut's hair (her previously immaculate French plait is now falling out in all directions and I'm pretty certain she has ice cream smeared across her left cheek). She takes my hand and, along with the other nannies and their charges, we are led back into the living room. I try not to gasp out load, but I'm not sure I do a great job as Alexa grabs my hands and squeezes it as if to say, *Calm down, this is completely normal.*

Sitting in the middle of the room is one of the most famous rock stars from the sixties. Despite almost certainly now being in his eighties, he is still wearing a tattered leather jacket and various tattoos decorate his forearms and neck. He is balancing an electric guitar on his knee and pulls his dark glasses down onto his nose as we all enter.

'Grandad!' one of the little boys, who I think is called Hunter, throws himself at the rock star and pulls his sunglasses from his face, promptly placing them on the bridge of his own nose.

The rock star laughs and ruffles his hair affectionately. I'm so star-struck, I don't know what to do. Here I am, about to do a toddler music class, with one of the greatest rock stars in the world.

Oh my goodness, my dad would be so impressed!

Alexa prods me in the ribs and I look around to see that the rest of the nannies are now sitting in a circle on the floor around the rock star, toddlers on their laps. In front of them are small bags of instruments. I follow their lead and place Coconut down on my folded legs, letting her rifle through the bag.

Five minutes later and we are all singing along to 'Wheels On The Bus' led by a bona-fide rock god. If I could tell you I have ever been in a more surreal experience I would, but this honestly tops it. As Coconut happily bashes two tambourines together and I try to remember the words for the song (plus the actions – the nannies know the actions!), I cast my eyes around the room.

More parents have arrived and it seems the celebrity status has doubled tenfold. I spot a beautiful British actress throwing her head back in laughter at the guy currently in the running for the next Bond. In the corner, a very famous member of a girl band patiently plaits her daughter's hair whilst simultaneously glancing at her BlackBerry. I inhale deeply, then exhale, before joining in with the next verse of the song.

This is just so surreal. Sometimes I really do think I have the best job in the world.

* * *

I flopped into bed at ten that evening, completely exhausted from the day's activities. After our singing class, I was instructed to take Coconut to a vegan restaurant in Notting Hill for her lunch. We were then driven halfway across London to Hampstead, where she had a private swimming lesson in the pool of an ex-Olympian swimmer. I was introduced to staff member after staff member when we eventually fell into the Aisles' house at 5pm (so many, in fact, that I found it impossible to remember names) before I was told that Mr and Mrs Aisles were impressed with my work today and were happy for me to get on with finding them a nanny – regardless of the fact I hadn't met them yet.

'They are very private,' explained Mila as she nodded at the butler to hand me my coat at the end of the day. 'Maybe tomorrow they will call to discuss requirements but if not, everything is in the file.'

She flicked her finger in the direction of my handbag, which was currently holding two lever arch files full of rules, job descriptions and the CVs of some nannies recommended by some of the Aisles' friends. I waved goodbye to Coconut, who had peeked through the curtains, her face flushed with tears when she realised I wasn't going to be her next nanny/partner in crime. I must admit, even I had a lump in my throat as my Uber drove down the road away from the house.

That little girl had just stolen a piece of my heart.

Having checked on a sleeping Rupert, I pulled my duvet up around me, laid out all of the files on my bed and reached for my glasses. Patrick was working abroad so I had our bedroom to myself, meaning I could sit up in bed this evening and start learning as much as I could about what the Aisles wanted.

Casting my eyes over the two files that Mila had handed me that afternoon, I was instead drawn to the scruffy little notebook Alexa had bestowed on me when we were chatting with the other nannies.

'Guard it with your life,' she warned as she handed it to me. 'There are some top nanny secrets in there.'

I had nodded and promised to return it to her as soon as I could, thanking her profusely for being so kind in lending it to me. I think she realised I had been given a pretty huge task in finding a new nanny for this family, and she – and the other nannies – wanted to help as much as possible.

So I turned to the first page and started reading. The headline, written in scruffy scrawl in a red biro simply said, 'The rules of a celebrity nanny':

1. **Put most of your personal life on hold.** Loneliness is guaranteed with many high-profile jobs and many celebrities will presume that their family is now your family so don't expect much of a social life.
2. **Make great friendships with the other staff.** Here is a list to consider: housekeepers, butlers, maids, masseurs, bodyguards, security guards, chauffeurs, tutors, chefs, managers. They understand what you're going through much better than anyone 'on the outside' and

can give you hints on how to cope with certain celebrity behaviour – these people are your allies!

3. **Be prepared to move to a new country at a moment's notice.** Most celebrities don't like to plan. If they wish to go to France for the weekend, then they go. But we all have to go too! You could call it exciting, which it can be, but with two toddlers and a baby to care for and making sure you have all their needs as well as your own, you must be prepared to be flexible and keep that smile well and truly planted on your face.

4. **Give social media a wide berth.** Talking of temptation, this is one area to be very wary of. Your privacy and the privacy of your employers is extremely important. It is vital that you keep it that way.

5. **Make sure you don't look like the nanny.** Some famous parents will instruct you to keep a low profile when the cameras are clicking. Why would they need a nanny? They can do EVERYTHING without the help of anyone, of course! Be prepared to always make it look as though the celebrity is doing everything themselves. If you spot paparazzi, step back so that you are out of shot.

6. **Get some defensive driving lessons.** You may have to become a decoy for a parent trying to escape some unwanted photo shoots and when you're being chased by unrelenting photographers, knowing the car you're in and how to drive it is so important.

7. **Don't even think about having a partner.** Nannies in relationships are frowned upon as it means there might be

someone in the mix more important than the children. You're best to remain single.

8. **Be prepared to fix every problem before the parent knows it's a problem.**

9. **Things to demand in your contract:** All food/drink, living arrangements, living expenses, holiday visas, a car with insurance, travel insurance, regular plane tickets back to your home (if you live abroad), a personal trainer (should the family want you to look a certain way), clothes allowance.

10. **You will be forced to have MI6/FBI-grade background checks.** That means DBS checks, references, interviews and even drug tests are all done before you meet the celebrity.

11. **You Have to Live the Same Lifestyle as The Celebrity Mummy.** If the family don't eat wheat, dairy or sugar and ban alcohol and coffee from their home, you'll have to be on board with this too.

12. **You won't be allowed a mobile phone.** Magazines will pay thousands for photos of celebrity kids, so it's easier to have a strict phone ban. That means checking your phone and electronics in at the door.

13. **Don't let a child repeat an outfit twice.** Sometimes it's useful to make a note of what they're wearing each day, so they don't get papped in the same outfit.

I sigh and pick up my pen, reaching for the first CV in my pile. *I've a feeling tonight's going to be a long night.*

Chapter 25

It was one of those days when my phone didn't stop ringing. Rupert was a year old and life had never been busier. We had decided to move out of London to the Cotswolds (something we had dreamt of doing for years and then realised we NEEDED to do once Rupert starting walking). I was surrounded by cardboard boxes, trying to pack as efficiently as possible whilst also trying to entertain my little boy. I peered around the corner of the kitchen island to see if my latest plan had worked – it had! My little boy was happily positioned in front of the washing machine, watching the pile of dirty laundry I had just put in whirl and disappear in the water.

Who needs expensive baby toys?

'Hello?' Trying to sound as professional as possible (and not like a frazzled mummy mid-boxing her London life away) I picked up my mobile phone.

'I found your website and was wondering if you could help me?' A clipped British accent came through the phone and I could tell the request was going to be an interesting one. 'I'm not yet pregnant, but I want to book a maternity nurse.'

For those of you not in the know, a maternity nurse is someone who comes to help look after you and your baby once you leave hospital. They can be absolute lifesavers to some parents who like the idea of having a baby expert in the house who can also help with feeding the child or answering any questions they might have.

I stall slightly before answering:

'Sorry, did you say you're not yet pregnant?'

'Yes, that's right. I hope to be pregnant in the next month or so and I wanted to book someone immediately.'

I peer over at Rupert to check he's still OK and then heave myself up off the floor to sit at the kitchen table.

'Sorry, can I take your name?'

'It's Amisha.'

'Lovely to meet you. Now, I don't know how much you know about maternity nurses but usually women wait until they are at least 12 weeks pregnant or more before actually booking one. That's because they usually arrive when the baby is born, so without a due date they will be pretty impossible to book.'

I hear Amisha sigh down the phone. 'But I heard that in order to get the best, you have to book ASAP. A friend of mine whose children go to school in Knightsbridge said there's only one maternity nurse she would ever book and all the mothers at school fought over her. She ended up having a year's waiting list.'

'There are plenty of amazing maternity nurses out there—' I start to explain, but Amisha cuts me off.

'But I need this very specific one. It will make the other mothers so jealous if I land her and they don't.'

Ah, competitive parenting. Amongst certain classes there seems to be an 'only the best' attitude, which is fine in itself, but sometimes the competitiveness over who actually has the best can get a bit extreme. This point was made even clearer when I received my second phone call of the day.

'He did it! He bought it for me . . .' Lisa was a client who I had been working with for a few months and she was constantly complaining to me about how annoying her husband was. By 'annoying', I think she means 'He won't get me everything I demand' but following this phone conversation, I realised she was obviously very good at getting her own way.

'He got me the Ferrari for the school run!' she gushed down the phone. 'The other mothers are going to be green with envy when they spot me and little Mikey arrive at the school gates. All of Mikey's friends will be so jealous!'

I 'congratulated' her and decided there was no point in reminding her that she practically lived next door to her son's school, so the school 'run' could have actually been done on foot.

With Rupert now bouncing away happily in his 'circle of neglect', aka a plastic Jumperoo that plays tinny music and flashing lights, the doorbell rings and I jump to my feet, praying it's the removal men.

'Special delivery. Sign here please.' I take the cardboard box, scribble my name on the plastic divide offered me and take the package into the living room. After kicking away mounds of bubble wrap and taking some boxes off the sofa and placing them on the floor, I sit down and open the package.

Wow, they really did do a good job!

I pull out the brown and beige dress with matching brown hat and white gloves and sigh.

Verity will love it.

I snap a photo and send it via WhatsApp to her.

* * *

Verity is a client with two toddler twins, who had contacted me a couple of months ago to help find her a nanny. Her list was extensive: fluent in French, skier, good cook. But there was one word on the list that had been circled in red pen which I couldn't ignore: *Norlander.*

A Norland Nanny is often considered the cream of the crop when it comes to nannying. Norland is a prestigious nanny college in Bath, where young girls train to degree level to be a career nanny. Not only do they have extensive childcare and newborn training, but due to often being hired by celebrities or members of the royal family, they are also taught martial arts, cooking (on an AGA, no less) and extreme driving skills (so they can dodge the paparazzi). Despite interviewing numerous nannies, Verity was adamant that she had to have a Norlander. The problem was, no Norlander was applying for the job. This might have been because she only wanted someone for two days a week, or the fact the salary she was willing to pay wasn't huge, but no matter how many calls I put into Norland, they were unable to send anyone our way.

'I think if your client could offer more days' work or a more competitive salary, then some of the nannies might be interested,' explained a tired-sounding secretary at the college. 'But at the moment, no one has applied for the position.'

Determined not to fail, I had managed to find Verity a nanny who I thought was as good – if not better – than a Norlander. She had 15 years' experience of working with toddlers, a degree in childcare and incredible references from all of her previous families. But there was one problem . . .

'She's not a Norlander, though.' Verity threw her hands up in the air and sighed loudly. 'I've told all my friends we're getting a Norlander. I don't want to be the only family in our area without one.'

Eventually, Verity hit on an 'amazing' plan, which she shouted down the phone to me at 2am.

'Sorry for waking you, but I've just thought: we can always dress that nanny you found me in a replica Norland outfit. That way, no one need ever know!'

Presuming Verity had had a few too many after-work drinks, I told her I'd call her back in the morning. On the phone to Verity the next day, I had managed to convince her she really didn't need a Norland dress to justify the standard of her nanny. However, a few hours later, whilst browsing eBay, I had to stifle a laugh as I came across a replica Norland fancy dress outfit for just five pounds.

I swiftly pressed 'buy' and couldn't wait to send it across to Verity with a cheeky note attached. I'm not sure her nanny will ever forgive me!

* * *

I must admit, there are times when I wish parents would just look around and realise there is no need to be competitive. But a bit like football teams entering a big stadium, some new mothers tend to puff out their chests and barge into parenting all guns (and wallets) blazing, reaching for the Best Parent Award with open arms. The competitiveness doesn't end at the children, though. I have had fathers literally wave their credit cards at me and demand I suggest 'the most expensive push present possible' for their wife. For those of you who don't know, a push present is essentially a reward for giving birth. In my experience, it's a man's way of saying, 'My darling, you have pushed a baby out of your vagina and now I shall shower you with thousands.' Push presents are something I'm asked about regularly, thanks to lots of women's magazines now pushing them (literally) as a must-have for any new mother. There are some beautiful and thoughtful gifts one might buy for a new mother – I still gaze down in awe at my amazing fingerprint necklace that Patrick bought me when Rupert was born, which has his tiny fingerprint engraved in it. Then there are also some 'gifts' that can get a bit excessive. Such as the house in the Maldives one client bought for his wife as a thank you for giving him a son, or the diamond choker rumoured to have cost over half a million pounds!

Some clients have also been more than generous with me when it comes to thank-you gifts. I must admit, I'm pretty old-fashioned at heart and I would never expect anything more than a lovely little thank-you card, but when a chauffeur arrived on my doorstop one morning, long legs folding out of his Bentley to present me with a little red box, I honestly didn't know what to expect. I read the note attached – a heartfelt page of thanks, which actually made me well up. It was from a client of mine who had had a baby through surrogacy and they had written the note on the way to the airport to fly to America to meet their little one. The ink was actually smudged slightly, which I can only presume was from tears of excitement that their baby dream was about to become a reality.

But it was when I opened the box that I actually stumbled backwards (and bumped my foot on the doorstep!) in shock: inside was a gold and silver Cartier watch. I turned it over in my hands, looking up to see the chauffeur pull away into the traffic before I could stop him and double-check this really was meant for me. When I turned it over, I could see that this wasn't a mistake: my initials had even been engraved into it.

PART EIGHT

TODDLERDOM

Chapter 26

I reach into the boot of my car and gather up a collection of files, being careful not to drop them. The back seat of the car is jam-packed with a collection of party decorations. I have 2,000 pastel pink and yellow balloons, a helium pump, party hats, multi-coloured streamers and a huge 'Happy Birthday' sign. Rupert is being looked after by our nanny at home. Katherine (or Kiki, as she is known) was a complete lifesaver for us when Rupert was little. If ever there was a real-life Mary Poppins, then she was it and I felt completely at ease when she looked after our son.

I breathe a sigh of relief as I spot the lorry appear at the front of the expansive drive and I wave manically at Michael the driver.

'You made it! I was having panic attacks on the motorway that you'd got lost.'

Michael grunts at me in return (he's not a man of many words) and walks around to the back of the lorry before opening the doors to the back, hands on hips as he shakes his head in dismay.

'You've got people to help with this, right?' he calls back over his shoulder.

At that moment, I hear a squeal from the front of the estate and Marjorie bounds down the stairs. Marjorie is my client and mummy to twin toddler boys, whose party it is today. At this estate. Which looks like Buckingham Palace.

'You're here! So, what do you think of the house? It's amazing, isn't it? Perfect for my two little princes!'

I turn around and, open-mouthed, take in the building in front of me.

'The nannies have all arrived and are waiting for you in the ballroom for their brief . . .' Marjorie walks down the front stairs towards me, looking as though she has lived in this setting her entire life. A tight cream cashmere sweater is offset by a set of pearls around her neck and a long, metallic silver skirt swishes around her ankles.

Goodness, I hope I look like that when I have toddlers, I think in admiration.

'The caterers are lost somewhere on the M4 – if you can find out what their situation is please – and the event planners are currently assembling the balloon arch.' She peers over my shoulder at Michael, who is currently unloading around 40 silver glitter balls and a gold and red velvet throne.

* * *

When I took on this job two months ago, I had no idea the extent Marjorie would go to in order to create the 'perfect toddler birthday party' for her twin boys. I have helped mothers plan numerous birthday parties before – sometimes doing it all myself, other times bringing in event planners if the parents want something a bit more unique. The second Marjorie told me her wish list, I knew I was going to have to bring in the big guns. At our first meeting, I met her in a little coffee shop to go through potential venues. Having not really had much of a brief from her at this stage, I had a list of places that I knew were 'toddler-friendly' but also had something a bit different about them – a private members' club in Soho which had a jungle-themed room, the possibility of hiring out the Disney Store for a Disney-themed party and if the weather looked good, the option of decorating a private garden square in Kensington with a vintage fairground theme.

But Marjorie took out a red pen from her handbag and swiftly drew red lines through all of my suggestions:

'I need something bigger and better than this. Here's my ideas.'

At that point she pulled out a huge laminated file and turned a few pages before pushing it under my nose. 'Something like this could work. Or maybe this one?'

I cast my eyes over the images in front of me. The first was of Highclere, the beautiful estate where the TV series *Downton Abbey* was filmed. The second photo was of an incredibly well-known castle in Scotland.

'Marjorie, this location is in Scotland. Do you think your friends would travel all that way for a birthday party?'

'When they see the sort of party I want to put on, of course they will!' She threw her head back in laughter and diamonds sparkled on her fingers as she ran them through her beautifully highlighted hair.

When we had our second meeting a week later, I was more prepared. This time I put the glossy photographs down on the table in front of her.

'What about this location? It's not far from London, sits on the Thames and it's absolutely perfect for a Narnia-themed party.' The theme had been emailed to me the night before – at 2am. (My work phone stays resolutely on by my bedside table, much to my husband's dismay.) I pulled up the Pinterest page I had put together, showcasing décor ideas, colour themes and entertainment.

'I'm going to be honest with you. To pull off what you want, we're going to have to bring in some experts.' I opened a new tab on my laptop to show her the website of London's most sought-after event planner. 'This is the guy we need to hire. I'll do all the liaising, make sure he knows what we want. You can now just sit back and relax; it's all taken care of.'

Marjorie flopped back in her chair and exhaled loudly. 'Oh, thank God!' she exclaimed, her Russian accent more pronounced now that she was relaxed. 'It's all in your hands, Tiffany. Don't bugger it up!'

'Just one more question . . .'

(I'm always nervous asking as I hate talking about money.)

'You're going to ask about my budget? There is none. Just make this the greatest party a toddler has ever had.'

With that, she waltzed out of the café, leaving a trail of Chanel perfume in her wake.

* * *

Arranging this birthday party had to be one of the more stressful jobs I've ever taken on. With every suggestion I put to Marjorie, her demands grew larger (more balloons, a bigger venue, Michelin-starred chef to cater for the parents!). Armed with my notebook and pen, I gradually managed to tick everything off her list, whilst keeping my head as calm as possible.

Which is why I now find myself standing outside this exquisite country estate ready to put the weeks of planning into action. First off, the childcare. I head determinedly to the ballroom.

The ballroom is one of those rooms that every young girl has imagined herself being waltzed around by her very own Prince Charming. The domed ceiling fills the room with wintry sunlight and rainbows of colour dart off each duck egg-painted wall. At the far end, a selection of women in their twenties and thirties are gathered, sipping cups of tea and talking quietly amongst themselves.

'Erm . . . Hello?' I clap my hands together (channelling my old school headmistress) and wait for the chatter to die down. Ten expectant faces turn towards me. 'Hi.' I clear my throat and try to sound confident. 'I'm Tiffany, the Mummy Concierge. I've spoken to you all at various times over the last couple of weeks and it's great you're all here.'

No one speaks. A couple of the women smile encouragingly, so I continue. 'Obviously, this is a slightly unique situation we are all in.' Quiet laughter fills the room as everyone nods and acknowledges that this is certainly not something they have ever done before. 'I've been through all of your CVs and interviewed you all personally, so I know you're up for the job. In about two hours, 100 little people will be descending on us and it's your job as our nanny team to make sure they're all happy, fed, watered . . . and that's just the parents!'

There are polite giggles again so I decide now to change tack: *why am I trying to be someone I'm not?*

'OK, enough with the formalities.' I gesture for everyone to come over to where I am and we all sit cross-legged on the floor. 'I know you are all mega-experienced and will do an amazing job. Let's just say I don't think any of us will have ever seen a toddler birthday party like this before, so if any of you have any questions or are worried about anything, just ask away. I'm basically here to make everyone's life easier.'

A couple of the nannies enquire as to which loos the toddlers can use (we have specific loos for adults and children – the adult ones are filled with Jo Malone candles and posh handwash, whereas the toddler loos have multi-coloured loo roll and soap that squirts out of a duck's beak. One nanny gestures towards a bag and asks if she needs to wear her official uniform. Her name is Emily and she trained at the respected Norland Nanny College – which has its own uniform complete with white gloves and a hat that the nannies are encouraged to wear. I smile back at her kindly. 'Only if you want to, but I think you look perfectly fine in your jeans and T-shirt.'

I hand out a list of names of all of the children who will be attending the party, alongside their assigned nanny, plus information on any food intolerances, play preferences and so on.

Right, nannies done. Now, onto the décor.

Running now (time seems to be passing very quickly), I venture into the second ballroom to find it has been transformed into a scene from Narnia. Fake snow lies on the ground, a glittering sleigh covered in icicles takes centre stage and actors dressed as Mr Tumnus and the White Witch mill about in the most extraordinary costumes I have ever seen. A snow machine blows delicate little snowflakes through the air and classical music plays in the background. I see Vincent, the event planner, in the far-left corner, talking animatedly with one of his assistants.

'Wow, this looks just incredible!' I throw my arms out wide and shake my head in amazement.

'You haven't seen the walk-in wardrobe yet ... Oh, there it is!' Vincent grabs my elbow and ushers me towards the door where a huge pile of fur coats is being wheeled in by an intern. 'We're going to transform this main door into a wardrobe so that the children have to walk through the coats to get to Narnia.'

He says 'Narnia' with a swoop of his arm and I feel a surge of excitement zoom through my body.

My goodness, this really is going to be the most incredible party ever!

Excusing myself, I head towards the estate kitchens, where a team of highly trained chefs are putting the finishing touches to a Narnia-inspired feast. There are cupcakes made to look like lions' heads, sandwiches elegantly resting on mini lampposts covered in snow and platters of Turkish delight sprinkled with blue and silver glitter. (There are also other foods specifically labelled for gluten-free children, celiac, vegan and so on – the chefs have thought of everything.) On a grand, thick oak table at the end of the room, there are menus printed on parchment detailing the options for parents. The parents, incidentally, are having a four-course sit-down meal whilst their children are entertained by the nannies and our troupe of actors, and they're indulging in Lobster Bisque, Beef Wellington and what look like expensive bottles of French champagne. My stomach rumbles as I survey the feasts, so I sneak a piece of Turkish delight from one of the bowls near me and pop it in my mouth – divine!

The brief I was given by Marjorie when we first met was to create a party that served a dual purpose: to engage and excite the children and surprise and delight the parents simultaneously. I look around again – I think we have achieved this perfectly.

'There you are!'

I turn to see Marjorie grappling with the twins (both dressed in velvet suits and bow ties, little gold crowns on their heads). She passes one of them – Henry, I think – over to me and I tickle him, making him explode with laughter.

'Is everything done? Are we ready to go? The chauffeurs should be arriving in around 15 minutes, so we need the nannies outside, ready and waiting.'

I nod and try to concentrate as Henry sticks his finger up my nose.

'This is all for you!' I tell him, gesturing towards the ball-room behind me and watching as Henry and his brother James' eyes open in awe as a life-size lion has just been wheeled into the house (goodness, it does look realistic . . .).

After I put Henry down, he laughs as he chases his brother into the ballroom containing all the fake snow. I hear shrieks of giggles and see them picking up handfuls and sprinkling it on each other's heads.

'I just have to hope the parents are as impressed . . .' Marjorie fidgets with the engagement ring on her finger and looks around. I can tell she's stressed, but who wouldn't be? She has pretty much emptied her bank account to put on this party.

'How could they not be?' I say softly, placing a reassuring hand on her shoulder. 'Look at the boys' little faces! This is literally a dream turned into reality for them.'

* * *

This certainly isn't the first time I have worked with competitive parents. Just like Marjorie, there seems to be a tribe of new mothers and fathers who treat parenting like a professional sport. The second their baby is born, it's as though there's a checklist of must-haves, must-dos and must-be-better-thans. At first, I was completely bemused by it all – why do these parents care so much about what other parents think? But the more I worked with people who live in a world of luxury, the more it started to settle on me that they are actually just like any other parent: they want the best for their child and they want to be seen to be doing the best. For some people, splashing money in order to do this might seem vulgar, but whenever I felt like this, I would take a step back and bring it back to the bare roots.

Every parent I have ever worked with who is competitive about the lifestyle they give their children is usually doing it because they want what's best for their little one. If a certain school has a reputation for being the best, why not give it your all to get your child in there? If you want to give your child a birthday party they will never forget (and you have the money to do so), who am I to say it's bad parenting? As my motto goes, every parent is different and every child is too. The only thing that's important is that YOU DO YOU!

I truly believe that with all of my heart.

Chapter 27

It's a breezy October morning, the kind where it looks as though England has decided to throw on its winter coat in a patchwork of reds, oranges and yellows and cover the ground and air in an autumnal haze. I kick up a bunch of soft leaves that have fallen to the ground and rock my arms merrily from side to side as I walk down a cobbled mews towards my first appointment for the day. The cold air catches in my throat and I pull my scarf up around my ears, but even that can't disguise the smile on my face. Whilst the rest of London are busy sweating on the Underground, their winter coats and hats being disregarded on tube seats as they reach the lower bowels of the city, I was one of those happy few actually looking forward to work that day. Why? Because I was visiting three of London's most elite members' clubs for children.

I'll be honest with you, when I first heard about a few new members' clubs for children popping up around the capital, I had to supress the mother of all eye-rolls. Why? Because when the emails first pinged into my inbox, I was hit with words such as 'Self-confidence classes for babies', 'Steiner-inspired art lessons' and 'Baby raves teamed with organic food'. Don't get me wrong, having lived in London for most of my life, I was used to hearing about the next weird and wacky craze that had descended on the city. In my twenties, I was one of the first people to test out a restaurant that hung 60ft in the air from a crane. In my thirties, when planning my wedding, I was invited to an exclusive wedding gallery, which was essentially like living inside the pages of a glossy bridal magazine (complete with perfumed rooms to match your mood). And now here I was, entering the exclusive realms of the parenting elite, and, I must admit, I was actually quite excited. According to my London Mummy set, Wind (aka the newest members' club for parents and children, which I've changed the name of because it's THAT exclusive) was THE place to be at the moment, so I had to be there – my job practically insisted.

A client of mine actually set the balls in motion after an initial phone chat with her, where I happened to mention the rise in children's members' clubs. 'I didn't even know they existed,' she said, sounding slightly put out. 'So, what do you have to do to get on the list? I presume there's some huge waiting list, right?' To be honest, at that stage I didn't know the answer, so I promised I'd find out and report back. Which is why I was standing in front of a tall glass building, decorated in butterflies, down a narrow mews in Notting Hill, off a side road adjacent to London's famed and beloved Portobello Road.

As I slid through the floor-to-ceiling doors, I was met by a slim, elegant woman, her hair in a top knot, who introduced herself as Ana. She was not what I had expected at all. She wore Lululemon yoga pants and had that clear porcelain complexion which meant there was no need for make-up. Her feet were completely bare and she had 20 or so woven bracelets decorating both of her wrists. If I could remove my surroundings and guess where this woman would be most at home, I would have said the long, sandy stretches of a Goan beach.

'Welcome.'

Her voice was like honey, a whisper compared to the loud and confident tones of the mummies I was used to working with. She took my hand and stroked it gently, looking me up and down in the sensual way that lots of hippy types do. Despite us being polar opposites, I immediately liked her. Her calm demeanour made me feel instantly relaxed and I felt the Zen fold itself into my body and any anger or tension melt away.

'Come, let me show you around and then I've booked you in for a complimentary massage. It's impossible to experience Wind without relaxing in Bali.' (By Bali, I realised she actually meant the luxury spa that was part of the club – aptly named because it was decorated in golds and peaches, with Buddha heads and incense sticks everywhere you turned.)

As I followed Ana down numerous corridors, I felt more as though I was in a luxury five-star hotel than a children's club. It was so far away from those dreaded indoor play centres parents begrudgingly trudge to on miserable winter days when the whole family has seen every episode of *Paw Patrol* ten times. Despite being slightly judgemental before I got there (I remember rolling my eyes at Patrick when I described where I was headed), I thought how much I wanted my child to come and spend time here. I mean, who wouldn't? I'd already been handed my 'Immuni-tea' (echinacea, hibiscus and cornsilk, in case you're curious) from a member of staff (who would have doubled as a supermodel) and all around me, I could see well-behaved children. Elbow-deep in paint and sequins, they are poised and happy, ready to create fridge-worthy masterpieces.

'It's so important for us as a club to find emotional and physical balance for everyone,' Ana explains, stroking the golden hair of a little boy as he calmly walks by. 'I want this to be a sanctuary for healing, relaxation and spending time with your loved ones.' The sense of calm is impressive. Despite the children chatting animatedly to each other and bursting into happy laughter, there's a calmness that seems to radiate from everyone.

I look down at the tea I'm drinking – have I been drugged?!

I nod open-mouthed and visibly impressed as Ana moves us from room to room. Wind is set over three floors – there's an interactive play-and-learn zone for families, a nutritionally focused plant-based organic brasserie, an onsite spa and salon and a holistic wellness clinic (specialising in everything from ayurvedic massage to cryotherapy). Obviously, I'm here to research the benefits of this club for children and babies (although I do feel a magnetic tug towards the spa) so I ask Ana to show me back to the ground floor, where most of the activities for little ones take place. The play area has a focus on sustainable toys and there are lots of wooden toys and games dotted around. Everywhere I look, there are babies and toddlers grinning with excitement and launching themselves at the huge ladybird that takes centre stage (and has been described by Ana as a sensory den). There's a pirate ship ball pit (currently expertly manned by a three-year-old and his teddy) and an impressive-looking treehouse (which looks like it has literally been plucked from a forest and placed inside). To the left, I see a children's café with handpainted walls depicting scenes from a woodland gathering. (I'm amused to see the menu is completely plant-based and wonder if I could ever convince my baby to indulge in 'cauliflower steak'.)

'We have weaning pots too.'

Ana has noticed that I'm looking over at the café and she picks up a small pot from a nearby fridge, which has 'Quinoa and beetroot' written on it. 'We completely understand that our members might have children of all ages, so we want to cater for everything.'

I can't resist poking my head into the children's bathrooms – and I'm not surprised by what I see. Unlike your average loo in a children's play centre, there are no discarded loo rolls or wet patches beneath the cistern. The bathrooms are instead themed like log cabins, with multi-coloured buckets for sinks. Even the babies' changing area stops me in my tracks. It has that stereotypical calm-like quality that oozes through the air conditioning of this club, and again looks like a mini spa for newborns. A circular changing area painted in calming whites and blues displays a plethora of cruelty-free and vegan baby toiletries – I wanted to clone it and take it home with me.

Ana softly takes my hand and nods towards a closed door before leaning forwards and opening it slightly. Inside, I see a children's class is running – eight little faces have their eyes closed in concentration as their teacher talks about mindfulness.

'We have lots of classes for the little ones. Heuristic sensorial singing class for babies, green classes which teach children about the importance of upcycling and recycling, Steiner-inspired art classes . . .' She stops and taps her finger on her cheek and I can see the Rolodex of classes spinning through her mind. 'Oh, and there's the string quartet class where children will learn to harmonise using the viola or violin – that's always a really popular one.'

I must admit, I don't know how to react. Steiner-inspired art classes – I'm pretty sure I was brought up watching Sooty and Sweep throw paint at each other on TV.

'So, how much is the membership here?' I've been wanting to ask this question for a while but haven't quite been able to find the moment. It feels almost brash to be talking about money and I feel slightly uncomfortable. I presume it's because the majority of mothers who come here probably don't even have to think twice about handing over their credit card.

'It's six thousand pounds a year.' Ana looks me directly in the eye as she says that, almost telepathically challenging me to have any sort of reaction. 'And all of our members are happy to pay this. After all, our spa speaks for itself – which you're about to see – and we have the best holistic experts in the world. Did you know our acupuncturist often treats Prince Harry and Meghan?'

I want to ask her who else frequents Wind (I'm sure this must be celebrity central) but know that Ana is far too discreet to divulge, so instead I follow her as we walk back up the stairs.

Whilst Wind's décor hinges largely on bright colours and loud patterns, stepping into their spa transports you to a calming space where you immediately feel the stress seep from your shoulders. Ana explains that she has booked me in for one of their signature treatments ('I never let a member leave this building unless they look as if they have just returned from three weeks in the Maldives'), so I take the robe she offers me gratefully and open the door to the spa changing room.

If I could scream in excitement, I would.

The doors to the changing room are hand-carved from Bali wood and even the towels are made from wood fibres. (How do I know this? There's a gold-framed sign that explains how the towels are biodegradable, therefore contributing to reforestation around Europe.) I start my 'relaxation session' by stepping into their Himalayan salt room, where you can sit and breathe opposite a wall of pink Himalayan salt. I'm then ushered quietly into a room to have a massage on one of their custom-made Dolomite quartz beds.

'They're filled with thousands of tiny, warm crystals,' my therapist explains, 'which work to reduce inflammation and promote healing.'

If I could tell you any more about my massage I would, but I was in such a state of deep relaxation that all I can report back is that one of those massages will be on my Christmas list every year.

An hour later, I feel like a changed woman and have to physically force myself towards the exit due to not wanting to leave. As I shuffle down the corridor, glancing wistfully at every massage room and wondering what bliss is happening inside, I bump into a tall, curly-haired woman holding a clipboard. 'Lovely to meet you – I'm Natasha, aka the colon whisperer. Make sure you come and see me next time you're here.'

I smile back and try not to convey any sense of horror on my face. *A colon whisperer? Goodness, this place really does have it all!*

PART NINE

THEY GROW UP SO FAST

Chapter 28

'It's really important to us that when Hugo grows up, he goes to Eton, then St Andrews, and therefore, it's imperative that he starts mixing with the "right" sort of children as soon as possible.'

I gulp down a mouthful of coffee quickly, scalding my throat as I do so. To say I'm in shock is an understatement, but in situations like this I need to remind myself that just because one parent wants something different to what you would want for your child, it doesn't mean they are wrong.

'And how old is Hugo now?' I ask cautiously, glancing sideways at the little boy sitting dressed head to toe in Ralph Lauren, his finger halfway up his nose.

'He's eight in April so we need to start quickly.' She sweeps a piece of paper across the table towards me and gestures at it with her diamond-encrusted finger. The words 'Etiquette Training for Little People' stare back up at me.

'This woman is supposed to be incredible. She was trained under a former member of the Queen's household and now lives in America. Apparently, she flies all over the world to teach etiquette classes and I want you to book her; I don't care how much it costs. I just need her here, in London, by next month.'

I'm pretty sure it's impossible to hide the bemused look on my face but I nod patiently and make a note of the etiquette guru's name.

* * *

A week later, and I have hit a wall: this particular etiquette coach apparently has a completely full diary until early the following year.

'You do know she has flown halfway across the world to work with celebrities and royalty,' quips her personal assistant when I eventually get hold of her. 'You really do need to be more organised to book her. She has a waiting list of over two thousand parents.'

I politely say goodbye and start working on Plan B. There's no way I can go back to my client and tell her I can't get her what she wants – I'm just going to have to look closer to home.

I'd heard about this particular etiquette academy through various Chelsea mummies who gossiped about it over skinny lattes and vegan cupcakes. It was a place that was often 'whispered' about, an 'in the know' secret that only the most exclusive of children has the privilege of being a part of. I pick up my phone and send a quick message to a colleague of mine who has talked about sending her eight-year-old daughter, Emma, to the academy. As luck would have it, her little girl is already enrolled on the six-week course and is halfway through. I politely ask if I might be able to tag along.

The following day, I arrive at Coworth Park hotel – a stunning luxury hotel in the Ascot countryside, Emma at my side and raring to go.

'Last week, we were taught all about how to dress for different social occasions,' she explains as she takes my hand and walks me into an elegant function room, where the class is being held. 'Did you know, you must never wear more than three colours at the same time?'

I look down at my multi-coloured shirt dress teamed with a slouchy blue blazer and a bright red scarf. Flinching slightly (and if I'm honest, nervous that one of the 12 eight-year-olds in the room might point out my fashion faux pas), I swiftly remove the scarf and jacket and stuff them into my handbag.

'This week is all about table manners,' Emma tells me, before bounding off to greet a friend that she has just spotted on the other side of the room. I must admit, I'm already impressed. When I first met Emma a couple of months ago at a dinner party her parents were holding, she had been a typically timid and shy eight-year-old who was barely able to whisper hello. In just three weeks, I can see how much she has transformed. She is engaging and articulate compared to many children her age who've already slipped into the monosyllabic awkwardness of adolescence. I watch, impressed, as she compliments her friend on her outfit and then engages in the sort of small talk that I only wish I could do – a part of me is tempted to pull out my notebook and take notes.

The class begins and I find myself a seat on the back wall so that I can observe. It's so easy to forget I'm actually here on 'work duties' and I have to keep reminding myself I'm due to report back to Maria about the academy and if it might work well for her son.

Two hours later, the class is nearing the end and the children are summoned to a beautifully decorated dining table in the centre of the room, complete with starched white linen table cloths, silver napkin rings and china teacups.

'We always get a meal at the end of each session,' Emma explains to me in that very grown-up way of hers. 'It's so that we can practise what we have learnt.'

The first course is soup and a smile breaks out across my face as I notice that each and every eight-year-old is eating their soup perfectly. Spoons swoosh quietly from the centre of the bowl to the top and there are no slurping sounds at all. I am equally impressed when the main course presents itself and I see piles of peas on the plate – not one child turns the fork upside down and scoops the peas. Instead, they spear the peas in small groups onto the tines of the fork using the back of the knife to help them. It's hard not to be impressed. Although it's easy to dismiss classes like this as something silly that rich people throw money at, I could actually see that there were some potential benefits for children in negotiating certain social situations in their lives, giving them the confidence and knowledge to do so.

* * *

The following day, my phone shrills loudly from inside my handbag. I reach down to retrieve it.

'So, what was it like? Will it work for Hugo?'

I swing open the door of the black cab and mouth 'thank you' to the driver before heaving all of my bags over my shoulder. I've just returned from a client who is due home any minute with her newborn baby. My job was to fill her home with flowers, make sure food was in the fridge and have all the baby kit up and running. I then had to rush to Waitrose before it closed to grab some food for supper.

I dump the bags on the pavement outside my house (I can't walk and talk at the same time) and concentrate on the voice coming through my mobile phone.

'It really must be up to the standard of the American woman otherwise it just won't work. Hugo needs the best and—'

'Maria, it was fantastic,' I tell her. I think back to the class I had attended the day before. 'Hugo will adore it and the teachers are wonderful. I definitely think you should sign him up.'

Maria stays on the phone to me for the next half an hour whilst I simultaneously unpack shopping and talk her through what the etiquette course covers. By the end of the phone call, I have managed to make a delicious-looking tuna salad and have convinced my client that the academy is an essential investment if she wants her little boy to have the manners of a prince.

Exhausted from such a long day, I finish the call, scoop the rest of the salad into my mouth and collapse into bed.

Another day in the life of The Mummy Concierge.

Chapter 29

The decision to try for another baby was not an easy one. Work was increasing hugely for me (which was fantastic), but there was also something niggling away at me that was making me wonder if I wanted Rupert to be an only child. Perhaps it was working with so many pregnant mothers or being contacted by clients who wanted help prepping for a second baby, but I found that every waking moment started to be filled with assessing the pros and cons of having another child.

Patrick was on board straight away (he's from a large Irish family and always talked about having a household filled with as many baby giggles as possible), but I carried on fluctuating between it being a great idea, or a really, really bad one. For starters, I hated being pregnant the first time.

I wish I could say I was one of those women who really embraced her swollen belly and could laugh at the fact she could no longer fit in her jeans, but that just wasn't me. Throughout my pregnancy with Rupert, I was crippled with anxiety that something might happen to the baby, or that I wouldn't be able to cope once the baby arrived, so for me, pregnancy was nine months of intense anxiousness.

Teamed with the knowledge of how hard it had been to actually get pregnant in the first place, I was also petrified that trying to get pregnant again might be futile – and this scared me the most.

For months, I agonised over whether I should stop taking the pill and if we should go down the rabbit hole of trying to conceive. Some days, I would look at how successful my business was and think, *How can I possibly do all of this with two children running around?* Other days, I would meet a pregnant client and see the excitement in their faces of a baby-filled future and crave it so intensely, I'd rush home to Patrick, declaring we had to start trying. But just when I thought I had made my mind up and was ready to commit to trying for baby number two, I was about to be hit with something that would change it all.

A gorgeous, sunshine-filled new client called Victoria had been emailing me for a few months for advice on conceiving as she and her husband were trying for their first baby. Obviously not a doctor so unable to offer her medical advice, we swapped emails where she bemoaned ovulation kits and asked for advice on how long they should be trying before they went to see a specialist. Her emails always made me smile – she was quick to laugh at herself and her lack of knowledge of anything baby-related (she even admitted she once thought a baby monitor was a TV especially for newborns so they could watch CBeebies!). She was one of those clients who I was convinced I would form a firm friendship with, regardless if she used me as her Mummy Concierge going forward.

Victoria had booked in to meet me for a coffee one afternoon in Kensington and I knew the second I saw her that she had news. She was smiling so much, her face actually looked as if it must be aching and she was clutching a brochure for a luxury baby brand tightly in her right hand.

'I need your advice,' she explained, having downed one cup of mint tea and promptly waving at the waiter to bring her another. That was another thing I noticed: she was unable to sit still. Every five minutes or so, she would be up on her feet, reaching for the sugar pot or dashing to the loo. She reminded me of an over-excited toddler and I just knew that the news she was about to share was going to be something positive.

'So . . .' She twirled her red hair around one of her fingers and her face exploded into a smile again. 'I'm pregnant . . .' I jumped up to congratulate her, but she motioned for me to sit down. 'But I have a confession first: I wasn't completely truthful to you in our emails.' Again, her expression reminded me of a two-year-old about to tell someone something serious about a broken tractor toy or a spilt orange juice. 'When I first emailed you, I said that Jake and I had only just started trying for a baby. It wasn't strictly true, we have actually been trying for two years.'

I tilt my head to the left slightly, confused as to why she felt she had to hide this from me.

'We were just so done with everyone asking us how we were doing and if this treatment or that treatment was working, so, when I contacted you, it was nice to just talk about getting pregnant like a normal mummy-to-be. It felt normal not having to talk to you about the tests we were going through and the ovulation predictors, etc.' She took my hand and looked me straight in the eye. 'So, I'm sorry, I hope you're not mad.'

I burst into laughter – it was impossible to feel anything other than happy around Victoria.

'Don't be so silly, Vic!' I squeeze around the table to give her a hug. 'You don't owe me an explanation. Getting pregnant and how you choose to do it is no one's business but your own. I'm just glad I could be there to make it a bit less stressful.'

'Well, that's the thing.' Her smile droops slightly but it reappears quickly. 'I'm only six weeks pregnant so it's *really* early days. We haven't told anyone – in fact, you're the only person who knows.'

I nod sagely. A lot of my clients are very wary about those first 12 weeks of being pregnant as a lot can happen and they feel they don't want to tempt fate by announcing the news and then finding that the pregnancy doesn't evolve.

Victoria ordered a croissant and I opted for a vast mug of coffee as we got down to business. Now that she was pregnant, she wanted to know everything, so before too long our coffee table was covered in pieces of paper sprawled in brightly coloured felt tip (it was all she could find in her handbag) with lists of antenatal classes, baby brands, pregnancy cushion recommendations and excuses for why she wasn't going to be drinking alcohol at numerous social occasions she had coming up.

'I just don't want people getting suspicious about why I'm not drinking and then realising that I'm pregnant. I want to tell them when it feels safe to do so. That makes sense, right?'

If I told you how many of my pregnant clients worried about being 'caught out' in those first few months of pregnancy, you'd laugh. The amount of conversations I have had revolving around 'reasons I'm not drinking alcohol' or 'clothes to disguise a baby bump' are enough to fill a whole magazine. Let's just say I certainly feel like an expert when it comes to giving out advice. So far on Victoria's list for being sober were excuses such as:

- 'I'm on antibiotics for a urine infection so can't drink' (no one ever wants to hear details about a urine infection, so this promptly stops any suspicions in their tracks).
- 'I've got the world's worst hangover from last night – I can barely keep water down' (another wonderful excuse that works well if you're suffering from morning sickness).
- 'I've got a huge work presentation tomorrow morning so I need to keep a clear head – but I'll be celebrating as soon as it's over' (I especially like this as it feels like

an 'in joke' – there certainly will be celebrations soon, but it will be when the announcement is revealed, rather than downing 12 Jager bombs celebratory-style).

- 'I'm doing "Sober October, Dry January, Dryathlon" . . .' (yup, I hadn't heard of that one until recently too, but apparently it's a new campaign where you can pick ANY month and remain sober – perfect if you're trying to disguise a pregnancy).

It's strange in a way, however, that I have a completely different perspective when it comes to those first 12 weeks of pregnancy. For me, keeping it a complete secret from friends and family has the opportunity of backfiring hugely if something were to go wrong with the pregnancy. I have had numerous clients who didn't tell a soul they were pregnant and then suffered a devastating miscarriage, meaning they had no one to turn to or look after them. They had done 12 weeks alone, without anyone knowing about the baby inside of them, and then they were left having to mourn the loss of that baby completely alone too. To me, that's just too heartbreaking to consider, so, when I was pregnant with Rupert, I told my closest friends and family members as soon as the line appeared on the pregnancy test, to ensure Patrick and I had the support should we need it if anything went wrong.

But things were very different for Victoria. A day before her 12-week scan, she called me in tears, begging me to go to her home. When I arrived, I was met by a crumpled, tiny version of Victoria I barely recognised. She was standing in her kitchen, tears streaming down her face as soon as I walked through the door. Jake, her husband, stood by her side, a heavy arm slumped over her shoulder, pulling her into him. His skin was pale and the bags under his eyes were evidence of stress and a lack of sleep. I moved swiftly, switching on the kettle and sweeping up some dead flowers from the vase on the sideboard into the bin – no one needed to be reminded of death at a time like this.

Taking Victoria's arm, I led her into the living room and placed a blanket around her shoulders. She held the steaming mug of tea in her hands and for a minute, I worried that it might be too hot, but she didn't care – I could see in her eyes that nothing mattered anymore.

Jake had filled me in on the phone earlier that day. Victoria had started bleeding a few days before and, concerned, they had ended up at their doctor's, who swiftly insisted on a scan. The scan showed a clear image of their baby, but there was no heartbeat. In one single swipe of a sonograph, Victoria and Jake's future had been crushed to the ground.

And in a cruel twist of fate, it just so happened that on that day, my life had changed too.

* * *

That morning, just two hours before the fateful call from Victoria, Patrick and I had concluded we *were* going to start trying for another baby. I had sat with him in bed, my list of pros and cons in one hand, and we had gone through each and every one, making sure that the decision we made was going to be the right one for us and Rupert.

The conclusion had actually been made when, after an hour of debating all pros and cons, Patrick had turned to me and said: 'It comes down to this – how would you *actually* feel if you knew you couldn't have another baby? Would it make you feel relieved, or sad?'

The word 'sad' had spilled out of my mouth before I even realised, and as I said it, I knew how true that was. The thought of *not* having another baby, of not holding a newborn or smelling that newborn smell was something I wasn't willing to never experience again. So, once all tea was drunk, we had happily concluded that baby number two was something we both wanted. I had actually skipped out of the bedroom, so excited by the prospect of expanding our family.

Then the phone had rung, and it was Victoria.

* * *

'Tell me what happened, but only if you want to talk about it,' I reassured Victoria, not wanting to pressurise her into going over all the details if she didn't want to. However, a part of me knew she would want to talk – I've worked with enough women who have suffered heartbreak through pregnancy, and in the end the majority of them *need* to talk about it. So that's when I sit and listen. I have to be their sounding board, their reassurance.

'I miscarried at the public pool two days ago.' Victoria talks quietly and thick, silent tears roll down her face. 'I was playing with my niece Evie in the paddling bit of the pool and I started to feel a stabbing, cramping sensation in my lower belly. I said to Jake, "Can you hold Evie? I think I'm having a miscarriage." And then I sat on the edge of the bench, lightly bleeding on a towel. I didn't know what to do.'

I sat and listened as Victoria went on to explain how everything had felt so surreal, as though she was looking down on herself and watching it all happen. Jake had scooped her up and, having dropped Evie back at his sister's, driven home because they had an Ocado delivery arriving and he didn't know how to cancel. I nod as she tells me this – so often partners have to put on a brave face and just take control in situations like this. People tend to forget that they are suffering from impending heartbreak too.

'Just as we were unlocking the front door, we heard someone say hello and turned to see two of our friends who lived a few doors down. It felt rude not to invite them in for a coffee, so on auto-pilot, we did. We sat and drank coffee and I continued to bleed.'

'Why didn't you go to the doctor?' I asked, horrified that Jake and Victoria hadn't acted sooner.

'I suppose I didn't want to accept what was happening. I sat there, talking about birthday parties and the latest Netflix drama, looking as though I didn't have a care in the world, whereas inside, my baby was dying.'

My hand flew to my mouth and I couldn't help but gasp. *Poor, poor Victoria, having to go through all this.*

'In the end, I turned to my friends and said, "By the way, I think I'm having a miscarriage",' she continued. 'No one really knew what to say. What are you supposed to do in that situation? Cancel your plans? Cry? I felt stuck in this place where I didn't want to upset anyone or make a bigger deal of it than it was. I was hugely aware that I wasn't quite 12 weeks pregnant and that lots of people miscarry before then.'

Victoria went on to explain that eventually Jake snapped out of his stupor and started acting like Superman – ushering their friends out, calling the doctor and walking her to the car. They drove straight to have a scan and the miscarriage was confirmed: there was no heartbeat.

Victoria was swiftly booked in to have a DNC, a process where they surgically remove the baby – 'I was awake the whole time and with every scrape, I knew they were scraping away my baby.' With that, she burst into tears. 'I don't think I can ever go through that again, Tiffany. I think I'm done. I can't be a mother if there's a chance of having to go through that again.'

* * *

Later that evening, I got into my car, having tucked Victoria in bed and given Jake strict instructions to call me if they needed anything. I knew, deep down, there was nothing I could actually do and perhaps having me around – someone who deals with pregnant mothers and babies – might be the worst thing for them both at that moment, but I needed to feel like I was doing something to help.

I opened my phone and clicked 'confirm' on the online order I had just placed. It might seem trivial, but when I first met Victoria, she had told me how much she loved a certain brand of shoes – for every shoe you bought, a pair of shoes was given to a child in need. To me, miscarriage is an impossible thing to deal with and the only way to survive is to take things slowly. I typed out a note to accompany the shoes I had just bought for Victoria and signed my name. *'One step at a time'* was all it said. That's all anyone can do who has suffered any kind of loss, I feel.

That night, I lay awake in bed for hours. What had happened to Victoria and Jake had really shaken me. I had come home from theirs and had numerous phone consultations with various mummies who were newly pregnant and excitedly planning their upcoming trimesters. Despite forcing myself to smile down the phone and answer their questions with enthusiasm, a real sense of worry had embedded itself in the pit of my stomach. Only that morning, Patrick and I had decided to start trying for baby number two and then five hours later, I was helping a mother mourn the loss of her child. It sounds so selfish to turn the situation around to me, but there was no denying it. I was suddenly feeling very scared: what if the same thing happened to us as had happened to Victoria and

Jake? What if we found it impossible to get pregnant and I had to face fertility treatment again? What if our baby was poorly, or worse still, didn't survive?

The anxiety rolled around in my stomach all evening. I pushed away the homemade lasagne Patrick had spent hours making and stared into the middle distance, not even able to laugh at my favourite comedy show on TV. People often think that because I work as a parenting expert, I'm devoid of worries – after all, I'm supposed to know everything there is about pregnancy and babies, so what could I possibly have to worry about? The truth is, I am also a woman. A woman who worries a lot, all the time. Having just seen the horror that Victoria had to go through, there was no denying the fact I was scared.

* * *

As the months rolled on, one of the things that started to really play on my mind was the actual conceiving bit. Having downloaded all of my concerns about miscarriages and a baby being unwell to Patrick and being reassured that we would do everything we could to keep happy and healthy and deal with whatever life threw at us in the best way we could, we started actively trying. At first it seemed almost 'fun' – that normal, carefree sex where you hope there might be a positive pregnancy test at the end of it. But then it turned into what I like to call 'Army sex' – named because it becomes so regimented.

Despite promising ourselves we could just 'see what happens' (couple language for 'let's just have sex and see if we miraculously do it on the right day/time and conceive a baby'), after a couple of 'not really trying' attempts, we then went all guns blazing. If we were going to do this, we were darn well going to do it properly!

Foreplay was replaced with various apps. Most couples have sex because they're horny. When you're trying for a baby, you have sex because an algorithm on an app has estimated your fertile window and a notification has popped up on your phone to tell you it's now or never. This notification doesn't care if you're tired/hungover/just had a screaming match with your other half – its sole purpose is to make sure you hop into bed that instant and try to conceive a baby.

A few weeks into 'App Gate', I felt the need to progress onto something more hardcore: the ovulation stick. Every morning, I would pee onto a stick and wait to see if a little smiley face popped up (an indication that it's time to get frisky). There were also the supplements – folic acid, Pregnacare vitamins, vitamin D – that I downed every morning whilst still in bed and almost before even opening my eyes. Then there was the 'flailing around on bed like an upturned beetle' which became a post-shag ritual, having read that sperm is more likely to reach an egg if your legs are in the air (Patrick found this equally horrifying and hysterical).

Every time I met with a pregnant client, I subtly started up a conversation about early pregnancy symptoms, grilling them about tender boobs (mine had felt a bit sore that morning in the shower) and morning sickness until I had completely convinced myself I MUST be pregnant (and that the sick feeling had nothing to do with downing three tequilas the night before in a rare 'sod this getting pregnant thing' act of defiance).

One of the things that really frustrated me when trying to conceive was the comments (usually from well-meaning friends) about it being the fun part. There were times when I wanted to upend my handbag onto the coffee table in front of them and watch their expression turn to one of horror as out came spilt ovulation tests, negative pregnancy tests and sperm-friendly lube (yup, don't go there!). Trying for a baby is HARD and I just wish more people would talk openly about it. Of course, there are the lucky ones who get pregnant on the first go, but for the majority of mothers I have worked with, trying for a baby is one of the hardest, most draining bits. There's a reason it's called 'trying' and that's because it really can become, well, trying!

Eight things you only know if you're trying to conceive

1. **Symptom spotting is a daily occurrence.** If you pee more at night, you wonder if a fertilised egg is pushing on your bladder already. If your tummy so much as rumbles then you consider morning sickness.

2. **You constantly fondle your boobs.** Yes, it's suddenly completely reasonable to grab your boobs at any moment and 'assess' them. Do they feel more tender than usual? Do I need a slightly bigger bra all of a sudden?

3. **You're no longer bothered about having *good* sex.** You just want it over and done with, as quickly as possible, at the RIGHT time of the month.

4. **Your period will become your tormentor.** You will dread it arriving every second of the day and will refuse to buy tampons until the very last minute (just in case . . .).

5. **You'll notice babies and pregnant women EVERY-WHERE.** On the bus, on the TV – hell, even Instagram will start targeting you with pregnancy ads!

6. **You will have a new shopping habit.** Sod that expensive face cleanser you used to buy, now all your money is being spent on ovulation kits and pregnancy tests.

7. **You'll become an expert.** You might have failed GCSE biology, but suddenly you know everything there is to know that was on the syllabus for reproduction.

8. **You'll become an over-sharer.** As your obsession with getting pregnant increases, you'll find yourself chatting away happily about cervical mucus and sperm quality.

Chapter 30

New parenting trends are something I have had to get used to in this industry. It certainly doesn't happen amongst all of my clients, but there's a fair few who have definitely taken it to the extremes. It was December in London and trying to fit in a couple of social engagements whilst in the capital before heading home for Christmas, a group of my friends and I (who all happened to work in the parenting industry) decided to meet one afternoon for hot chocolate and mulled wine. We were lifelong friends, one of whom worked as a maternity nurse, there was a baby sleep expert, a couple of baby PRs and a couple of nannies too.

We walked along the Thames taking in the sights of the London Eye and all of the happy, smiling people stepping on and off it. Slightly further up, a couple of Christmas stalls that looked like mini chalets had been set up, selling toasted marshmallows, metallic Christmas baubles and nutcracker toys. We passed one particular stall that had been covered in fake snow and had an archway of bright pink baubles leading up to it. There were mini reindeer toys dotted around the scene and fake snow was being blown from what must have been a wind machine behind the stall – it looked completely magical.

'Oh, goodness! Influencer alert . . .' Christine the maternity nurse nudged me in the ribs and looked over haughtily towards a small child and her mother. I looked back at her in confusion. Influencers to my mind were skinny teenagers dressed in tiny hot pants wearing far too much make-up, pouting into their mobile phones, but looking around, I couldn't see one anywhere.

'There,' Christine stage-whispered back at me and turned my body around so that I was facing the mother and her baby again – in squint in case I missed something.

Just as I was about to protest – I couldn't see an influencer anywhere – the mother picked up her toddler, who I could now see was dressed head to toe in Burberry, and placed her under the bauble arch. The toddler tottered slightly (this could have been because of her fur-lined boots, or simply the fact that she was only just learning how to walk) and then turned to her mother and pouted.

Flash! The light from her mother's phone captured the picture perfectly.

'Darling, say something to the camera, sweetie. Can you say "snow"? That's it, show Mumma your Burberry bag.'

I watched entranced.

'It's insane, isn't it?' said Alexa, joining Christine and me whilst blowing on her mulled wine. 'I've worked with so many mums who have turned their children into mini-influencers. Some of them have over 20,000 followers and they're not even six months old.'

'A client I once worked with used to earn hundreds of pounds every time she posted a photo of her baby at a luxury hotel,' quipped Monica, one of the nannies. 'Quite a few of their friends got in on it too and before we knew it, Baby Bay had seven friends who were also baby influencers. I think their parents got pretty competitive about who got the most "likes".'

'I met some porcupine parents the other day at a job interview,' said Emma, the youngest member of our group, who had just made the switch from au pairing to nannying.

We all exploded into fits of giggles.

'Porcupine parents? What the hell does that mean?'

'Well, they're the type who coordinate their wardrobe around wraps, slings and other baby-wearing devices and use terms like EBF [exclusive breastfeeding] and assume everyone knows what you mean.'

'Yes, they're the type of mums who give their children kale chips and know great placenta recipes.' We all grimaced at this. 'They sew cloth nappies, home school, co-sleep until the child is 11 . . .'

'I think it's awful that people always put labels on parents,' Alexa chimed in. She is one of the more sensible ones in our group – I love her for it – as she's constantly sticking up for mums, no matter what.

But Christine ignored her – she was on a roll.

'What about period parties? Have you heard of them? A friend told me a mum from school held a period party for her 13-year-old. She invited all of her daughter's friends round to celebrate her first period, complete with red-themed food and drink!'

We spent the rest of the afternoon picking up stocking presents and filling ourselves to the brim with hot chocolate and marshmallows, before hugging goodbye on the Southbank. I decided to walk along the Thames for a bit before heading home. I was feeling nostalgic for my family Christmas – I would head home to my parents and my mother and I would sit in my bedroom on Christmas Eve, wrapping up all of the presents and chatting until the early hours. Then, without fail, my mother would leave the room demanding I get into bed and ten minutes later, a slightly wobbly (let's blame it on the Prosecco drinking during Christmas wrapping) Father Christmas would emerge – ho ho ho-ing and delivering stockings around the house. My mother's father used to do it when she was little and the tradition has continued ever since. Christmas Eve wouldn't be the same without a red-clad member of the family, a pillow up their sweater, delivering stockings.

It's funny how, when you're pregnant, you think about your upbringing and your relationship with your parents so much. Walking along, watching the street lamps silently flicker with the background noise of a slightly-too-merry Christmas party singing carols as they exited the pub, I gently placed my hand on my newly pregnant tummy.

'I'll make sure I give you the best Christmases ever,' I promise. 'We will dance around to musicals and look out the window for Father Christmas and squeal with delight when it snows. I promise.' I wiped a silent, happy tear away from under my eyelashes. 'I'll be the best mummy I can ever be to you, just like mine is to me.'

Conclusion:
Bumps, Babies and Beyond

A few weeks ago, I had one of those days. Work was busy, which in theory was great, but it also meant I was putting intense pressure on myself to divide my time equally between my clients and Rupert and Patrick, whilst also trying not to overdo it as I was six months pregnant. I swore (loudly), fed Rupert baked beans for lunch and then pretended it was his bedtime an hour before it actually was.

It was only when I sat down at 10pm with a hot cup of tea that my thoughts started to beat me up.

Was I a bad mummy? Should I really be trying to run a business when I could be spending more time with Rupert before baby number two arrived?

Like an old-fashioned slide show, memories of the last couple of months, subtitled with 'you are a bad mother', started to flicker across my brain. I remembered the day I ran into the kitchen, late for a meeting with a newly pregnant client, and Rupert's face had lit up, the words pouring from his mouth with excitement: 'Are we going to the park?' He had noticed I had my shoes on and was reaching for the car keys. 'You can watch me on the swing and we can slide down the big slide together.' His crumpled, tear-stained face when I explained I had to go to work will stay with me forever.

I also thought back to the day Patrick and I went in for one of our first scans for baby number two. Despite being so excited that Patrick joked I was like a Jack-in-the-box, I remember the sense of guilt that sat in the pit of my stomach as I saw the tiny image of our baby flash up on the scan.

How could I ever love this baby as much as Rupert? Was it wrong for me to bring another baby into the world, when I didn't think I could love anyone quite as much as I did our little boy?

Thrusting my shoulders backwards and switching off the TV, I marched upstairs and snuck into Rupert's nursery. The scene could have melted anyone's heart – his hair was plastered to his face and the pillow had left little indents on his skin, which actually looked like miniature hearts. He was clutching Blue Blue (the blue rabbit he had had since birth) so tightly to his chest that I could see it move as he breathed. In his left hand was the dinosaur toy that I had given him a few weeks before, refusing, as he so often did now, to let it out of his sight (despite the fact it growled every time it moved, meaning it regularly woke him in the night). Stroking his hot, soft skin, I reached down and planted a kiss on his forehead, breathing him in as I did so. But the subtitle appeared in my brain again: *Am I a bad mummy?*

That's when I decided to confront this thought head-on. I had heard about and read about mummy guilt, but this was getting ridiculous. Could I no longer enjoy even a night-time kiss with my baby boy without challenging myself?

Leaving Rupert's room (making sure the door was held half-open with the hedgehog-shaped doorstop and that the night light was on in the corridor), I found my laptop in the kitchen and opened it up, carefully typing in the name of a parenting expert I had read about in the newspaper. Clicking on her website, I located the original article I had seen and began re-reading it. One sentence really stood out: 'Think about your other friends and how they look after their child. Think of specific scenarios that they have done and ask yourself, "Do you think they are a bad mother?"'

I took out a pen and wrote down a list:

- My best friend's four-year-old still has a dummy. Does that mean he will still have it when he goes to university and that she's a bad mother? No.
- Some mothers put their babies to sleep in their own room after six months. Does this mean they don't love their children? No, of course not.
- Some mummies scroll through their Instagram instead of listening to their toddlers (minute-by-minute) account of what just happened on *Paw Patrol*. Does that mean they're not interested in their child? No.
- Some mummies co-sleep. Some mummies use full-time nannies. Some mummies feed their babies Ella's Kitchen pouches instead of cooking fresh organic meals

700 times a week. DOES THAT MAKE THEM A BAD MUMMY? Absolutely bloody not!

- Motherhood is HARD. We are all doing the best we can, in the way that works for us. So, if you feed your baby formula because it means your partner can do a bottle and you can have a glass of wine, go for it. If you need to sit your toddler down in front of Peppa and George so you can actually put some make-up on, then do it.

As I stopped writing my list and re-read everything that was on the piece of paper in front of me, it hit me there and then: when you become a mummy, EVERYTHING becomes about your children. These little things (the choices you make every day, just to make your life a little bit easier) are absolutely fine to do. You will worry that things you do might be wrong or someone else might be doing something better or just different to you. But that worry just proves what an amazing mummy you are. Some people like to judge you for the choices that you make. Some people will tell you that the way you parent is wrong and that the choices you make are not right. But in that instance, I decided something. I would say: SOD THEM AND TELL THEM TO BUGGER OFF! What you're doing is enough. You are an amazing mummy. Every mummy is different and every mummy is nailing motherhood in their own individual way.

Myself included.

* * *

Two months later, I was eight months pregnant. I had taken a day off to spend time with my mother who was visiting whilst Patrick worked away in London. I'd promised her that my work phone was turned off (it wasn't – it was on vibrate in my handbag) and so we headed for a lunch of sushi in the sunshine. We began chatting about numerous 'birth stories' that we had heard.

'Did you know that your grandfather delivered me on the bathroom floor?' My mother raised her eyebrow in expectation of my reaction.

'What? Pop delivered you? Are you *serious*?'

'I think my arrival was a bit of a surprise. I've always loved a bit of drama!'

At the time, my mother's comment didn't mean that much to me, but I look back now and giggle every time I think of it because of what was about to come.

Later that evening, my mother and I had just put Rupert to bed when she looked at me strangely as I slowly closed his bedroom door.

'Are you OK?'

I realised I was grimacing slightly and holding on to my stomach.

'Yes, just slight tummy cramps. I think I'm going to have a bath.'

I'll be honest with you, at no point did I ever think I was going into labour. I was only eight months pregnant and wasn't due to have my C-section for at least another three weeks. But something inside me made me text my obstetrician anyway. I've always been the nervous type so the last thing I expected was a barrage of questions and then a text response that said, 'Get in the car asap and get to the hospital. I'll meet you there.'

What ensued was an hour of panic, including dramatic phone calls to Patrick – who was already on the train back to the Cotswolds – to explain that the second he arrived, we would be jumping in the car and driving straight back to London. The pains in my stomach were getting stronger but, having never had contractions before, I was still just convinced these were Braxton Hicks (false labour pains some women experience in their final trimester). There was no part of me, at all, that thought I would be having a baby that day. Call it ignorance or fear, but my brain refused to even digest it as a thought. As far as I was concerned, we were going to the hospital to be checked over and I would be back home in no time.

Kissing a sleeping Rupert on the head, I stood in his bedroom for a few minutes, breathing deeply. Then, I jutted my chin out, grabbed my hospital bag (just in case – as a Mummy Concierge, I'm always prepared!) and jumped in the car. The main thing I remember is my mum waving lamb chops at me (that she had cooked for our supper, but we hadn't had time to eat), asking if I wanted her to wrap them in tin foil for the journey!

The car journey was horrific. I had always been nervous that living an hour and a half from London, yet planning to have our baby in the city, something could go wrong and I'd end up giving birth on the M4.

And that's nearly what happened.

* * *

'How's the pain, darling?' Patrick sounded calm and in control but inside I knew he was nervous. There was his wife sitting next to him, a contraction timer on her phone, writhing around in agony every couple of minutes. As soon as we had got into the car, we called our obstetrician, who confirmed to me, she thought I was in labour: 'Just breathe deeply and get here as quickly as you can.'

It was now around eleven at night and the dappled lights of the street lamps reflected onto puddles in the road. I tried desperately to concentrate on the sounds of Classic FM that were filling the car, rather than the pains in my stomach.

'Oh my God, what was that?' Terror completely engulfed me as I felt a pop in my stomach that made me double over in pain. 'Patrick, I'm scared. Something just happened. We need to get to the hospital.'

Pulling into the underground car park – usually swathed with cars but now eerily empty – I jumped out of the car only to feel a huge gush of water between my legs.

'It's my waters, they've broken! Oh my God, we're going to have the baby in this car park!'

Patrick scooped me up in his arms and pushed the button to the lift furiously.

The doors to the hospital swung open and I felt myself in the arms of a midwife. Immediately, I started to relax. It was OK, I was safe. The next half an hour was a blur of hospital gowns, midwives, a quick 'hello' from Natasha the obstetrician before she disappeared into the operating theatre and frantic phone calls to our family.

We were going to have our baby – now!

Despite going into labour and being 7cm dilated, I was still able to have a C-section. I remember being wheeled down to the theatre with memories of Rupert's birth intertwined with the reality of what was currently happening. Everything was slightly more rushed this time – I was later told that I actually had an emergency C-section – but a strange sense of ease fell over me as I knew what to expect and what was going to happen.

As the numbness travelled up my body, thanks to the spinal drip, I lay on the theatre table and tried to concentrate on what was happening. I knew from last time that the doctors would tell me when they were going to start, i.e. make the first cut, and that usually, all being well, my baby would be in my arms within five minutes.

Closing my eyes, I started to count.

One minute . . .

I felt Patrick's hand squeeze mine and I opened my eyes briefly to catch his reassuring smile.

Two minutes . . .

My mind flicked back to Rupert's birth and what it had felt like when he was shown to me for the first time. How my life had changed instantaneously and had become so much richer and worthwhile in that simple second.

Four minutes . . .

A collage of images flashed across my eyes – the women I had worked with over the last years, their babies, the relief on their faces when I assured them it would be OK. That first text message I'd receive, announcing their little one had arrived. The moment their lives changed forever.

Five minutes . . .

And here she was. I saw my little Ophelia for the first time as they brought the medical drapes down and I heard her tiny cry. Within seconds, she was lying on my chest, blowing bubbles from her lips and I felt it again: that momentous moment that will never become any less magical no matter how many times you do it: I am a mother. *A mother!*

To me, motherhood is the single most important role any human will ever play in the life of another. Nothing else can produce the joy or broken heart that motherhood allows. Motherhood is walking around with literally all of your nerve endings raw and exposed. There will be days when you want to give up, when you are just too physically tired and you wish for the life you had before children. But there are also days when you have never felt happiness like it. I love that at the age of 38, I can fly a kite whilst squealing with joy, blow raspberries, pretend to be a dinosaur, decorate pavements with chalk, eat cake covered in Smarties, observe ants, play catch, build cities in the sandbox and laugh hysterically, constantly.

When Ophelia turned one, I remember overhearing Rupert console her over a broken toy tea cup – 'Don't worry, Mummy can fix it. She can fix anything.' It was one of those moments when the world slowed down around me as the words flitted through the air. Looking over at my small son, gently stroking his sister's hair and reassuring her 'Mummy can fix it' proved to me just how much your role as a mother can literally change your little ones' lives.

You are not just a mother. You are not just someone who cooks and changes nappies and gets cross at bedtime. You're not just someone who sits up until the early hours when your child has a cough and measures out doses of Calpol whilst stroking tired heads. You're not just someone who magically turns into a dragon and rescues numerous princesses from towers. You're not just a sandwich maker, a bath runner, a plaster applier or a cuddle giver. You're so much more than that. To your little ones, you are a superhero. You can fix anything. And who doesn't want to be Batman?

Useful Resources

The Baby Book: How to Enjoy Year One by
Rachel Waddilove
www.rachelsbabies.com/my-books
This book was my absolute saviour when I was a
clueless first-time mummy – Rachel's advice is sensible,
heartfelt and achievable (plus, she is one of the nicest
women I know!). The routines she suggests for you and
your baby are flexible and easy to follow (no matter how
sleep-deprived you are!).

**Your Baby Week by Week: The Ultimate Guide to
Caring for Your New Baby** by Simone Cave and
Dr Caroline Fertleman
This book is a lifesaver! There are a couple of pages on
each week about what to expect in terms of crying/sleeping/
feeding, etc. It's not a parenting guide, it just tells you what
to expect that particular week.

Happy Mum, Happy Baby: My Adventures Into Motherhood by Giovanna Fletcher

A wonderfully candid insight into celebrity mummy Giovanna's own personal experiences during pregnancy and motherhood that makes you realise no matter who you are, motherhood and pregnancy come with the same stresses, pains and laugh-out-loud moments.

The Wonder Weeks: How to Stimulate Your Baby's Mental Development and Help Him Turn His 10 Predictable, Great, Fussy Phases into Magical Leaps Forward by Hetty Van der Rijt, Frans Plooij and Xaviera Plas-Plooij

Have you ever wondered what's going on in your baby's head? Why is a normally well-tempered baby suddenly difficult and demanding? And then, suddenly, he is doing things he could not do the day before. This baby development book explains how to stimulate your baby's development whilst also dealing with 'leaps' (translate as: times when they are a nightmare!). A really helpful guide that you can read weekly whilst your baby grows.

Secrets of the Mummy Concierge by Tiffany Norris

Well, it's a MUST-HAVE for any pregnant or new mummy, right?

Acknowledgements

Would you believe me if I said I found these acknowledgements to be the hardest part of this whole book to write? As someone who always wanted to be an author, acknowledgements were always the first thing I read when I opened a new book, so in truth I've been dreading writing these because I know there are so many people I should be thanking – people who have shaped my life and helped me become me.

But I've decided to keep this short.

First, an enormous thank you to Natasha Singh at Chelsea and Westminster Hospital – my incredible obstetrician who delivered all of my babies, but also made sure I was OK when tough times hit. You saved me from turning into a gibbering mess when times were hard and I'll never forget your comforting hugs when I needed them the most. Also, some of our WhatsApp chats keep me smiling even to this day. Did I really message you asking if a 'throbbing big toe could be a sign of labour'?

A huge thank you to Jo Bell, my literary agent and one of the kindest, most softly spoken women I know. You were the person at the end of the phone when I was told I had a book deal and I will never forget that moment! It was one I had dreamt about for years! Thank you for trusting that people would want to read this book and for encouraging me along the way. You enabled me to achieve a life-long ambition and I'll always remember that.

To Beth Eynon, my wonderful editor. I'll never forget that day during Lockdown when I heard you wanted to publish my book (read as: Best. Day. Ever!). Thank you for believing in me and for your constant support. Some of the wonderful things you said about my book make me want to print them out and frame them! I couldn't have asked for a kinder, more talented editor. And to the team at Bonnier, who have put so much hard work into this book, a huge, heartfelt thank you.

To all the mummies out there who I have worked with over the years (and all the mummies to come). Thank you for letting me help you during the most important times of your lives.

To *my* mummy: thank you for always supporting my 'crazy ideas' (proposal planner, undercover bridesmaid, Mummy Concierge!) and for being on hand with a bottle of pink prosecco when occasions came to celebrate. If I'm even half the mummy to Rupert, Ophelia and 'Baby Number Three' as you are to me, then it will be my greatest achievement in life.

Daddy, you know I couldn't have done this without you. You may have raised your eyebrows at times and thought, *What's she up to now?* But I did it! Thank you for being there in my lowest moments (and sending me on a late-life ski season to Verbier, which literally changed my life!). You have supported me in ways I shall never forget.

Everyone has an angel in their life and Amanda is certainly mine. You really don't know how much you mean to me. Every time I talk to you on the phone, I end up smiling and I have to pinch myself at how lucky I got to have you as my big sister. I just hope Ophelia and her little sister have the same bond and friendship that we do. And to Elliot, the master of getting babies to take their first steps, there's another one coming your way soon, so you'd better start training!

And finally, Patrick: you always believed in me – more so than anyone else – and so this book is, in truth, thanks to you. You made my dreams come true in every possible way. In you, I have met my husband, the most incredible father to our children and the person I can never be without. Know that I will love you till the end. LYMAMED;-)